CLACKAMAS LITERARY REVIEW

2012
Volume XVI

Clackamas Community College
Oregon City, Oregon

CLACKAMAS LITERARY REVIEW

Editor in Chief
Ryan Davis

Associate Editors
Trevor Dodge   Emily Pass
Matthew Warren   Charis Woodward

Assistant Editors

Stephen Ford	Heather Frazier	Dana Harding
Caitlan Honer	Sandra Junda Matson	Heather Pinto
Ryan Rau	Ashlii Szocinski	Lee White

Clackamas Community College English Department

Cover Art
Colette Fallon
"Columbia River Pilot"

Journal Design
Matthew Warren

The Clackamas Literary Review is published annually at Clackamas Community College. Manuscripts are read from September 1st to January 31st and will not be returned. By submitting your work to *CLR*, you indicate your consent for us to publish that work in print and online. This issue is $10; issues I–XI are $6 if ordered through *CLR*; issues XII–XV are available through your favorite online bookseller.

Clackamas Literary Review
19600 Molalla Avenue, Oregon City, Oregon 97045
ISBN: 978-0-9796882-4-9
Printed by Lightning Source
www.clackamasliteraryreview.org

CONTENTS

Editor in Chief's Note

In 1997, with the support of the Clackamas Community College English Department, Jeff Knorr and Tim Schell created *Clackamas Literary Review*. Over the years and under the guidance of many editors, the voice of *CLR* has shifted subtly. Some years, we may have been seen as a poetry journal, while in others, a journal dedicated to fiction. In 2001, Tim wrote "that the mission [of *CLR* at the beginning] was obvious: create a literary journal that would publish the best literature we could find regardless of who wrote it." While the editors have changed, we want to reiterate our stance: *CLR* will always strive to offer the finest essays, fiction, and poetry to its readers.

Thank you,
Ryan Davis
Editor in Chief

The Poetry Teacher

Jack Powers

In the great poetry factories of China,
I tell my students, *each poet,*
must produce a poem every ten minutes.

Students hunch over blue-lined papers.
They clutch pens like wild quills.

Randall Jarrett, I say, *said poets*
stand in thunderstorms
hoping to get hit
five or six times in their lives.

But the room is cold, say the students
and the water colder.

We are seeding the clouds, I say,
We are speeding the clashing fronts
We are standing to our hips in water.

They scribble furiously.

Our factory is a ship, I say
hunting for storms in the sea.
I roll marbles in each hand
to trouble their cadence.
See the lightning in the distance!

But we are sinking, say the students

You must learn to swim, I say,
To breathe under water.

Glub glub, say the students

The fish have little flippers, I say,
and the ocean is vast.

Water magnifies their panicked faces.

Don't flail your arms, I say,
but they can't hear me.

I squint against the shock of lightning
illuminating skeletons of mackerel,
of students floundering against the black sea.

White paper rectangles rise, furl, unfurl.
Pens sink like harpoons into the deep.

I forgot to tell them
about surprise. *None for the writer,*
I say, but it's too late.

The bell rings and they must go on
to Calculus, to History.

End with an image, I say,
but their pens are capped.
They clutch their backpacks and chat
as they paddle toward shore.

Moments of Light

Eric le Fatte

Lying in my bedroom
beside you, and dreaming
about you, I surfaced across
the boundary of sleep
to reconfigure
the flight path of my dream,
which had veered
just a few degrees
from the landing
I had in mind.

Through the window
the moon threw
a huge yellow glow
As though it were
dissolving in clouds,
and the beams fell to earth
to soften your face.

A moment later, I perceived
what had seemed to be lunar
was composed

less of the moon
and more of the light
from a lamppost,
positioned so as
to illuminate
the empty street.

I'm sorry it wasn't the moon.

Whose Face

Jean Esteve

Suppose his face his face don't please
    my jaded eyes when waiting's done.
suppose his own eyes hold a cloud
    of counterfeit gone seasons

and his hands stay by his side
    while mine fray, fray handkerchiefs,
there we stand gaining time
    for what next mischief of our gods—

tell me, sure, his feet don't sink
    down in slime like treachery
or that his toes don't curl around
    mine and say we're both betrayed.

I will sleep I will sleep with my hogs instead
of that boy whose face I don't find splendid.

Blackberries

If, then, we are to be poor,
let us do it in perfect squalor.
Let our kitchen swarm with cockroaches
and blackberries have at our yard,

Don't work happy
but pouring sweat
and desire for our iron bed.

If, then, we are to be poor,
let the nails spring loose from our front stoop,
where we can face each other naked,
swaying, bramble-scratched.

Mo Chroí
(Irish Gaelic for 'my dear', literally 'my heart')

Ruth Beck

The damp air curls
through the lace of
pre-dawn Small Town
on a Sunday morning.

Bodies sleep in their beds,
hibernating,
while the last lost rays of day
break pinholes through
construction paper cornflower
blue black night.

As I walk, *mo chroí,*
my fingers unlock the sash
of each closed window. I turn
the deadbolt on every door,

placed like a sentinel

in this dark quiet,
climb the stairs where

even floorboards speak
a saturated language all their own.

It is here I find you
in your bed;
alone, unguarded
by the warmth that is
uniquely yours,

silent unmovable self,
mo chroí,
in each and every breath,
behind each window
unreflecting.

The Wake Fields

If your voice was not
familiar as in dreams or daily
phone calls, I could re-forget
your smoke-pressed rivers until shadows
gathered again.

This hedge cut
rained on quiet would not
reach its leaves toward that
answering room you painted
full with sea shells, abalone, red wine—

all I am needing.

Nothing real has come out of me
since I saw you; the light
inside your glowing window lamp
is the wanderlust
in everyone's eyes.

Though
there has been all last Autumn

to remember
and forget, and the rocks
to soften beneath the lap of the water gods,
I know it's over, really
over now.

The music of your laughter,
silenced,
till it was heard in the mistake
of listening when a voice in the park was
not you but other, pitch-bent,
haunted, stole from me that secret:
how to live again.

This whole world is wayfaring; you
see what lies ahead as the *filidh* churns
the unforgiving omen, exhumes
the madness of the waves that call
forever and do not return, and
are not enough.
In the turn of your page
a fog drifted into my hands
and laid my heart on your breast
like some wounded animal. The river
as I leave you collapses
on over under itself in a blackness
through the threshold door, a river
inside a river inside flowing.

Your face takes shape
in its own evening weight; I
smooth its frailty away. You
change by what I forget now
into the liquid vague of a year,
but when the garden is crowded
with sunflowers, and Autumn deepens
its hold, I will remember only
by your telling me—

On a storm singed day,
when sleep full women are dreaming
in fire lit houses I shall know
what you meant when you said
you dreamed my becoming as the apple
dreams in the twinkle of an eye.

Thursday night, the baby sleeping

Fullness
does not always depend
on a round belly,
an armload of firewood,
cups running over.

It is sometimes
in the secret joy
of being known,
wanted,
cried out for.

It is
    lingering
in the sweet ache
of desire,

unremorseful,
the honest need
for another.

Credit Check

Peter Serchuk

The rich don't love money.
They fear its ghost more
than the ghost in heaven.
Like chocolate, once the taste
has made a home in your mouth,
the terror of its absence
is the sweat in twisted sheets.
The poor don't fear money or its ghost.
They can barely remember its face
like some neighbor who moves in
one week and out the next.
As for me, money and I are lovers
although our affections often stray.
We bribe each other with promises
of hotel suites and philanthropy.
We share vows at the bank
and hold hands in secret pockets.
We promise till debt do us part,
our fingers crossed, knowing
even good hearts are sometimes

paper-thin and all that remains
are memories of Presidents
and mountains of IOUs.

Provoking the Bull

Rick Marlatt

As punishment for this and burying
the Ford in the mud like a stiff
collie
my brother and I circled the dining
room
in a slow, mindless
dervish,
matching napkin to plate, spoon to
knife,
pouring water as ice cubes tinkled and danced.

I admit it was probably me who
brushed
his shoulder when we crossed
paths.
The quick thrust of his knuckles into my chest
felt like the squeeze of an electric
fence.
I vowed to scissor his Sabbath CD to
slivers.

He promised to drown my baseball glove in motor
oil.
I said I could never love him.

He told me I didn't look like dad.
The fork left my hand before I knew I threw
it.
I remember the lack of sound, the bizarre sight

of the silver prongs finding their soft target
between his forearm and bicep, the impossible odds.
He stood near the window in the swelter of a moment,
amber light glistening off his beading forehead,

the unnatural limb of silver extending from his body,
something terrible quaking inside of him,

his eyes burning like a pair of scarlet suns,

brothers erupting in the immovable dusk.

This Blue Dress

America Marie

There were days with you, in this blue dress.

We took a drive to the beach and I was happy and comfortable,
wearing this blue dress.

I sprinted down to the water and you admired my youth.
I felt alive and kicked water at your feet.

Laughing, you sat down in the wet sand and watched me
as I twirled and cartwheeled and raced for your approval.

So many things we never said to each other,
but we shared that beach,
with the reflections of clouds on the wet sand,
knowing we would never amount to anything.

These swirls of blue, Van Gogh's flowers,
make me happy when I look down.
My breasts look different now and my feet don't move as quickly
but we shared this dress,
that day
on the beach.

Grandpa Waiting

Warm, musty Buick on a late spring day,
bouncy blue fabric covered benchseat,
bobbly-headed dog shakes up and down and back and forth
on the window shelf,
nodding in approval with each bump and turn.

It takes twenty minutes to drive the six blocks home after school;
these are my favorite moments and they seem to last forever.
The stale smell of Old English is sweet on my Grandpa's breath
And I look up to little gray stubble and watery eyes
as he enjoys every click and return of
the massive steering wheel.
His only daily outing;
"enjoyment"
is an understatement.

Home again, home again "jiggety jig jig,"
he turns to me and winks.

It takes a while to situate his fake hips
as he prepares to let me out
before entering the narrow building;

a dilapidated remnant of a 60s handyman garage
that he takes much pride in.
I think I hear the grumpy possums turn over
and moan in their daytime slumber,
tucked under the cheap, holey plywood.
As I exit and wait,
he drives the smooth, white boat of a car
into the possum haven.

Grandpa makes his way out of the garage,
his metal hips lead
in front of a hundred pounds of old man bones
and the driveway gravel crunches under our
carefully paced feet—
He walks slowly because I am little
and I walk slowly because he is fragile.

Nobody Loves a Snowy Girl

David Harris Ebenbach

A lot of times it took Katie a minute of sitting in the big, wide parking lot at the end of the day before she could get out of her car and walk toward the elementary school building where the day care also was, that ugly box-building that looked a lot like the prison eight miles down the same highway. She sat with her hands on the wheel, and on the radio would be Bob Castor, the afternoon talk radio guy who was "the last and humblest defender of America." She had a feeling he was making a lot of things a little too simple, and he was not a nice guy, but she liked to use his voice, his certainty about who was right and who was wrong, to help gather the strength to go inside. There was something heavy—too heavy—about the building and what was inside. She saw the dull no-color of the concrete and just felt like she was under it.

"And so you've got these liberal people," Bob Castor was saying, "who think of the word family like it's a four letter word, these guys who would put their sons in dresses if the New York Times fashion pages told them to, who would sell their grandmothers to the Cubans for cigars, who would tack on an extra wife and a gay *life partner* and cite the Koran as their authority. I mean, that's what we're talking about, here, and I'd like to hear someone say something intelligent about it today on the phone lines." Katie knew that he was responding to something particular in the news, something that had happened today, but she had only been listening for a few minutes, and had missed the main issue. But the way he talked—it straightened her spine.

She turned off the radio and stared at the box of a building another few seconds before finally getting out of the car. Then she crossed the gray parking lot, feeling her exhaustion and the cold— November was bad this year—and went into the cement of the school building, down the dark hallways, thinking of caves like the ones they always used to talk about being in Afghanistan back when everybody was talking about Afghanistan, and then she opened the door to the room.

Immediately she was hit by the burst of sound from a bunch of four- and five-year-olds screaming. It was like a punch, almost. Breathing deeply, she spotted Lexie, her blonde hair loose from its ponytail, lying on the ground in her almost-new blue shirt and her blue skirt, mixed in with another girl and a boy, caught up in playing with some stuffed animals in the far corner, and she was steeling herself, was just about to go get her and then get out of there, when she was blocked by a girl she'd never seen before. This girl, around Katie's age, mid-twenties, but with black curly hair, stepped forward in a way that was a little bit of hesitating and a little bit of forceful.

"Ms. Turner?" the girl said, her hands behind her back.

"*Mrs.* Turner," Katie said, feeling some anger rise up in her before she could get it back down, turn it into a smile.

"Oh—I'm really sorry. My mistake," the girl said. She had an accent, a not-from-Indiana kind of accent, certainly not from southern Indiana, maybe an east coast kind of accent.

"It's okay. You can call me Katie, really. Mary calls me Katie." She pointed at Mary, who gave a wave from the other side of the room, and who was the main woman in charge of the four-and-five group.

"I'm Jen Shafer," this girl said, and she put out her hand for shaking. "I just started in your daughter's room." Katie took this in, worked more friendliness into her smile. "It's good to meet you," Jen Shafer said. She was a pretty girl, a little more tan than most people were by this time in the fall, a couple of dark freckles high up on her cheeks. "I was hoping we could talk a minute before you took Lexie home. Do you have a minute?" And already, as she was asking, she was moving them back. Before she knew it, Katie was out of the room again, the door closed.

"Is there a problem or something?" she said, feeling like she was in trouble somehow, looking up and down the hallway, which was empty but still close around, and the windows were caged in with wire so that no kids, she guessed, could just jump out, even though this was the first and only floor of the building.

Jen Shafer herself looked in both directions, and then, while Katie's heart tightened, pushed a chunk of black, curly hair back out of her face. "Well, first of all, I wanted to introduce myself," she said. "I haven't met you yet." She put out her hand again, and they shook again.

"It's nice to meet you," Katie said. Somewhere around a corner a door opened and closed. The sound of footsteps moving away.

"And I also wanted to talk to you about Lexie," Jen Shafer said, like she was just finishing a sentence that Katie had interrupted. "Like I say, I'm new, but I thought I should tell you what I've been observing this week."

Katie felt herself go tight again. Who was Jen Shafer, anyway, going around observing anything? Where was Mary?

"I'm not going to tell you anything you don't already know. Lexie is a great kid—so smart and so enthusiastic and so sensitive."

Katie relaxed, but only for a second, because Jen Shafer kept going, her nose wrinkled like she was embarrassed about what she was saying. "But I've been noticing how her energy can get a little out of control sometimes. I've been seeing her grabbing toys from the other kids, and even doing some shoving. And today she threw one of the blocks at me. I mean, it was a soft block, spongy," she rushed to add. "Don't worry about that. I just thought you should know." She pulled her hair back again. It just wouldn't stay out of the way. Jen Shafer waited a second for Katie to say something, and then said, "I'm worried about her aggressiveness."

"Her aggressiveness?" Katie finally asked. "But she's a five-year-old girl. You said she was sensitive."

"She is, Mrs. Turner, but—"

"*Katie*," Katie said, snapped. But she heard new footsteps in the hallway, coming toward them, and she flushed with embarrassment. Then, softer, "You don't have to use my last name."

"Okay," Jen Shafer said, nodding. "I just wanted to draw your attention to this. Like I say, Lexie is a great kid. I just wanted you to know about what I was seeing. I thought you could think about it. Maybe you would have some ideas about it." Another girl, maybe another mom, went past them up the hallway toward the other rooms.

"How come Mary never said anything?" Katie whispered, thinking, *Maybe it's you, New York girl. Maybe you're making it up.* And then she felt embarrassed thinking that.

"I don't know why," Jen Shafer said. The door opened behind her, and Tina, Sammy's mom, came out with her son.

"Hi, Katie," she said, all bright smile. Tina was a nice girl. She saw the conference going on and hurried her little boy down the hall.

Katie turned back, tried her best to try to put on that same kind of smile. "Thank you so much. I'm really sorry if Lexie has been a pain at all for you."

"It's okay," Jen Shafer said. "We don't have to turn this into a whole big thing. Why don't you go get Lexie. We can just all keep our eyes on it. Okay?"

"Sure," Katie said. Despite herself, she was thinking unsmiling thoughts. She went ahead of Jen Shafer back into the room and looked around for Lexie, who rushed over and wrapped Katie's legs up in her arms before they had even made eye contact. The room around was crazy with screaming kids, and here was this girl who loved her mother. Katie looked up and saw Mary smiling over at them. Over all the noise, Mary called, "How are things?" and Katie called back, "Just fine," even though she wasn't feeling fine, and that was all of that. Then she loosened her daughter's grip, and Lexie looked up at her with her Mommy's own green eyes, and they walked out of the room again without another look at Jen Shafer.

Still, in the car she asked Lexie about it. She had the volume on Bob Castor turned down, so that he was just this low kind of drumming sound in the background, and she said, "I met someone just now." There wasn't any answer, and she looked at her daughter in the rear-view mirror.

Lexie, sitting in her big-girl car seat, had her blonde hair forward over her shoulders, and she was playing with it in both hands. It was long enough that she was always playing with it.

"Lexie?" Katie tried again.

"You met someone, Mommy," Lexie said. She had this thing of repeating what you said sometimes, to show she was listening, but it sounded like she was running the conversation. Katie always got embarrassed when it happened out at the supermarket or the post office or somewhere like that.

"I met Miss Jen."

Lexie's eyes went up, met her mom's eyes in the rectangle of the mirror. It was hard to say what was in her mind.

"Miss Jen wanted to talk to me. What do you think she wanted to talk to me about?" Katie said.

Lexie gave a cautious shrug. "I don't know, Mommy," she said.

"Have you been behaving yourself in your room?" Katie looked out over the road, which was empty. "Playing nice with the other kids?" Bob Castor said something loud on the radio, yelled it, but she missed it anyway.

"Yes," Lexie said quietly.

Katie opened her mouth to ask something more about that, but a different question came out. "What do you think of Miss Jen?"

"She doesn't like me."

That could have been. Even with all that "great kid" stuff she had said, maybe Jen Shafer just didn't like Lexie. As far as Katie ever saw, Lexie was the good girl, the one who shared toys when she was supposed to, who always knew to say "nice to meet you" and "please" and "thank you." She had tea parties with imaginary people and was a really polite hostess. *Soooo nice to see you*, she'd say to her imaginary guests. *Have more. After you.* And now she was staring at her mother through the little mirror, her green eyes nervous.

"It's okay, baby. It's okay," Katie said. "Don't worry about that Miss Jen." The drumming of Bob Castor continued in a calmer way. She said, "Where's she from?"

Lexie sat back in her seat, relaxed a little, grabbed her hair again. "New York," she said. And then she started singing some made-up song, looking out the window at the highway as they passed a strip mall half-full of open stores and half full of ones that were boarded up. There was one store with a broken window, and Katie for a moment had an image of Lexie breaking it, throwing a fist-sized rock at the glass. Katie shook her head. That was what Jen Shafer had given her in two minutes—that image. She turned the radio up to clean her head out.

Elliston had never been a great town, as far as Katie knew. It was never a place where people got rich off of a mine or a well or an industry of some kind, and there was no big river, nothing historical to draw tourists. At one time, though, there had been jobs. There were two factories, both on the same end of town, one of which had made auto parts before it closed down, and one of which still made animal food for zoos and labs—on a day when the wind blew west you could smell that animal food smell—though they did their work with fewer and fewer employees.

Katie worked in a small store—convenience and drug—right on Main Street, a street that was really just a slow stretch of the State Road, rolling in one direction to the animal food factory and the closed-down auto parts factory and beyond, and in the other out toward the prison. There was still some life on Main—the City Hall was there, plus the biggest church, and the pizza place—but a lot of the rest of it was sitting empty. Most of what was left of Elliston was out on the edge of town now, in strip malls. Even the schools, that building they'd just been in and the high school, were out on the edge of town, and that was the beginning for some of the kids; those that were eventually going to leave for other places started getting restless just by making the daily trip to school. Katie had been making those trips in the passenger seat of her father's car a few years ago, the wind coming in through the leaky windows. She had leaned her cheek against the glass, the ice of the glass. Staring out the window at the banged-up houses on the side streets and along the State road, she had not been one of the ones who thought about getting out of there. Elliston had never been a great town, but she also had the sense that it would never go anywhere, never mess her up, never leave. That was something.

They left the car parked in Mr. Ray's driveway, and after looking up at the low sky—could be snow coming—they went up the steps to their second-floor apartment over Mr. Ray's garage, on Green Street. These stairs were another narrow place, nothing like Katie had imagined for herself when Mike was here and when she and Mike had been talking about the future. Lexie hopped up the steps, two-footed for each step, and Katie carried up her daughter's backpack and all her tiredness from work and all the weight of the day care center. Lexie had to hop back down as well as forward in order for her mother to keep up. Katie didn't think she felt as young as twenty-five was supposed to feel. Everyone told her that was young. "You've had trials," they said, "but you've got your whole life ahead of you."

"You're right about that," Katie would say.

On the way in the door they passed the official military photo portrait of Mike, there in the dark entranceway, his face still and serious and hard to recognize as the guy she'd known. He had been the kind of guy whose face was always on the move, talking or joking or worked up angry or something. "Hey, Mike," she said, touching the photo, like she usually did. Lexie just breezed past toward the living room. It had been a long time since that photo had meant much to her. "Can I turn on the TV?" she said, already turning it on. The sound of a cartoon started crashing and banging in there. Katie told her she could.

Katie was still standing in the entranceway. *That New York girl is talking about your daughter*, she said to him, in her head. He kept his face composed, still, serious. She had to do everything now—even be mad on Mike's behalf. She shook her head, went back to the mini-kitchen, and took a can of beer out of the refrigerator, looked out the window at what was definitely going to be snow.

Maybe she would keep Lexie home from day care tomorrow. There was the snow, and maybe it wasn't good for Lexie to be spending time with Jen Shafer anyway. Katie could call in sick herself. She couldn't afford to do that, and the whole week at day care was already paid for—for the millionth time, Katie wished her own parents could find a way to watch Lexie at least some of the time—but Katie thought she just might keep her home anyway.

"Do you want to stay home tomorrow?" she called out to the living room. "Lexie?"

"Stay home tomorrow?"

Katie went to stand at the doorway to the living room.

"You're not going to work?" Lexie said.

"Maybe not," Katie said.

Lexie smiled a little smile. Mary had never said anything about Lexie being a problem. Mary had been really nice when they lost Mike, and she had never, ever said anything about Lexie being a problem.

They spent the evening watching TV and slowly eating their dinners on the couch. Katie knew that it wasn't maybe what she was supposed to do as a mother—her own mother would be sure to tell her that, along with a bunch of other things—but Lexie had asked, and both of them had had a bad day, and this way they got to sit right next to each other instead of opposite one another at the table. The cartoons suited Katie's mood well enough. She pictured Jen Shafer saying, *You know, I think she's watching a lot of TV and I thought you should know,* and she imagined Bob Castor saying, *These liberal people think you don't know how to parent your own children!* and they just watched their shows and ate their dinner.

At one point, Lexie looked over at her mother and said, "What did Miss Jen say?"

Katie looked back at her, surprised. Her daughter's face had a defiant frown on it, a kind of challenge. Katie decided to let the challenge pass by. "It's not important, baby. Don't worry about it."

"Mm," Lexie said, and then she put her eyes back on the television.

When it was a little past the time Lexie was supposed to get to bed, they shut the TV off and Lexie got herself ready in the bathroom and then they sat together in the bedroom, Katie on the edge of the bed.

"You're really going to stay home tomorrow?" Lexie said.

Katie had to admit to herself that she wasn't as sure about it now as she had been earlier, but she said, "It sounds nice, doesn't it?"

"Mm," Lexie said.

Afterward, Katie settled into the couch, which was also her bedroom, and had another beer or two, and watched some more shows. For some reason she kept it on the cartoon channel, didn't feel motivated to change it.

Overnight the storm came in strong and she woke up to it: white thick over everything. She could tell just from the extra quiet outside, even before she got up off the couch and pulled the shade aside to see the still-dim street, barely marked with tires. Maybe five or six inches, it looked like. There was something nice about the way everything was quieted down like that. The world looked slow and easy.

The apartment was chaos in comparison—dinner's dishes on the carpet next to the couch, the beer cans on the water-stained coffee table, her work clothes over the back of a folding chair. Toys everywhere. The TV was muted but on, two animals arguing about something. Her own mother would look around at this place in disgust, and she would say it was Katie's responsibility to take care of it. *Your mess*, she'd say. *Your problem*. Katie thought about jumping out the window into the soft snow, but then with some determination turned the TV off and gathered everything else, throwing away the garbage and folding her clothes, straightening the pile of magazines and then tossing them out, too, after more thought. She wiped down the counter in the kitchen area, washed and dried the dishes. She put her shoes in the closet near the door. She found a box from a case of beer and began to fill it with the stuffed cats, the Barbie, the little doll clothes, and put all of it by the hall down to Lexie's room. Then she stopped. The carpet was still too many colors and she half-wanted to take down the ugly pictures of forests on the wall—they seemed ugly to her now—and just leave the one of Mike in the entranceway, but she saw that she was being a little nuts, and so she just went around the surfaces, dusting and wiping, and called it done.

Down the hall in her room, Lexie was asleep with her mouth open. She looked slow and easy, too. Katie just stood at the door and watched her daughter, sleeping with nothing to worry about. The room was crazy with bright drawings all across the floor, dolls, little sneakers, clothes, and here she was sleeping quietly in the middle of it. Katie set the beer case box down on the carpet, and even though it didn't make a sound as far as she could tell, Lexie lurched up in bed.

"*Oh no!*" she said, in a panic. "What happened?" Her eyes were wide, her hands on her mouth.

"It's okay, baby," Katie said, leaning tired against the door jamb. This was how waking up was for Lexie sometimes. "Nothing happened." Lexie's eyes slowly came to an understanding of the room. She closed her mouth, wiped it with the back of her hand.

"Mommy," she said. And then her little shy smile, the one that said she was out of that evil place between asleep and awake, that she was fully here now.

There was a little time before Katie had to really decide anything, so she took Lexie outside first thing to enjoy the snow. While they were getting their coats and boots on, Lexie said, "Are you really going to stay home today? Do I really get to stay home today?"

Katie opened her mouth and closed it, and then said, "You know, let's see."

Lexie's face squeezed a little in an unsure kind of way, but then she got back to the task of tugging at her boot.

Mr. Ray's house had a rough little yard in back, and he didn't mind if they used it whenever they wanted. Today it was rambling with snow, and they had to kick through drifts even to get around back to it.

"Wow," Lexie said. She was still young enough that this kind of thing was a big deal every time. "It's a lot." And then she dove in, scooping up snow and throwing it loose into the air. Katie stood back and watched it all snow down again, nice and bright with the sun really coming up now. Over and over Lexie did this, and then Katie said,

"Do you want to try to make some snowballs?" and they both tried it. The snow was a little too dry, but they managed to make a few, and they threw them at the one tree back there.

"That's the bad guy," Lexie said. "Get him."

"You got it," Katie said, though she wasn't picturing a him so much as a Jen Shafer. Either way, they kept missing.

"This is stupid," Lexie said, after one too many misses.

"Okay, well, what else do you want to do?"

Lexie didn't answer, just roamed off a few feet, crouching, her arms buried in the snow. She started to just toss it around, creating little new snowbursts in this direction and that. Katie looked up at the sky, which was heading for blue and clear. The morning was cold, cold, cold. She looked all around—at the little paved strip behind the yard, also covered in snow, the other houses, the glimpses of Green Street, not plowed but dug through by the force of cars that had already had to get somewhere. Those cars were gone, though, and the whole world was quiet and still. It was like there was nobody anywhere.

Suddenly she heard Lexie making a strange sound, and her eyes snapped back to her daughter, who was turned away. "Are you okay?" Katie said. Lexie just kept making that sound, not answering, so Katie went over to her, turned her to see. Lexie was holding up her mittened hands, and Katie saw that the mittens were too old and too small, and that there was snow all over them, and through them, and inside them, and she saw that the sound was Lexie crying. "Oh, baby," Katie said.

Lexie turned away harshly, moved a step from her mother. Katie went to her again. "Let's go inside, baby," she said.

"No," Lexie said sharply, hugging herself.

"Your hands are cold, Lexie. Let's go inside and warm up."

But she was crying so much, too much for just cold hands. She kept pulling away from Katie, and was now basically bawling.

Katie tried again. "Baby, what is it?"

Lexie said something too quiet to be heard, and when her mother asked her to repeat it, she said it a little louder. "Nobody loves a snowy girl," she said, turned all the way away.

Katie felt a swelling in her, around the surprise, the sweetness, of Lexie's words. She moved forward with determination now, turned Lexie, hugged her with a lot of strength. "I love a snowy girl," she said. "I love you."

But all of a sudden Lexie was saying "NO! NO, NO, NO!" and shoving at Katie, shoving her hard away. Katie let go in shock, fell back to sitting in the snow. Her daughter looked wild, her wet face twisted in anger. "NO!" she yelled. And then she was grabbing snow and rushing at Katie, was throwing it in her mother's face, smashing her face with snow and with mittened hands. Katie found herself scrambling backward, her hands up helplessly, until she was back against the house, until she had curled up to protect herself, her head between her knees. Still Lexie kept the barrage coming, kept it coming until she stopped.

Katie lifted her head, saw Lexie stomping off across the yard. She touched her own nose, knew that there was a little blood there. Lexie was pushing her way through the snow and then plunging her hands into a drift against the tree. Katie flinched, expecting more violence. And maybe it was violence—Lexie ripped furiously into the snow, threw snow off to both sides, and whether it was digging or punching Katie couldn't tell. She didn't get up to intervene. She just watched her daughter do it, whatever it was. There in the bright of the snowy morning Lexie dished out her punishment—against the cold, against the weather, against her mother and everything else—and Katie watched. She bled from her tender nose and she watched and she didn't intervene. In some sense she was rooting for that girl.

JOHN KEATS!!

Brandi George

Angel flowers in the dark above
           my bed like drops of blood
      in dishwater. He is light
        surging through eyes of mounted bucks
    on the walls of the room where
      my cousin and I hide
           under comforters. We sail
      through winking universes, write
our names on each other's backs.
      His wings—tidal waves, cellophane—scrape
        against peeling wallpaper,
           while we conjure all the promises
      our mothers do and do not keep.

Another dream where Keats leads me
    through the house where he grew up.
    There's a stone door in back of
    an apothecary room.

No one is around except us. Beyond
    the door there is an ancient, flooded forest.
    We swim through leaves. The clouds are
    also underwater, and

God is in all of it, shining beneath

Each tree as if the trunks are only shades
    over a bulb. *Here*

Lies one whose name was writ
    in water.

Mother told me I was afraid
            of the circle of light
hovering around me as I slept. But I don't remember
    anything except how I
            climbed into bed with her. I wish
    I were a ballerina again, always
    spinning too fast, the world a gash of paint.

In my childhood, there were four dreams:
        Covered in snakes, Mother reads
            by a lake of fire; Old Man bites
        my shoulders; Farmhouse falls
    into the ground; the porcelain cowgirl
            begins moving so I strangle her.

He says it's nothing personal—
    crackers and milk for dinner; hours

before the TV oracle; our bodies
      locked tight as remote controls against the night.

        I told the little girl we almost adopted,
        You can't see darkness with your eyes shut.
          But I had no advice about the bathtub, where
    her drug addict mother had held her under
          water until it broke upwards through her nose.

    Angel has grown good
with his purple eye and mess of air
    soft on my pillow. He slides
        into my chest and eats the bandages.

The wide world! I'll never
    trace the shore.
  I'll cease to be. Your shadow
    stands, a high romantic symbol
of love. Faces un-reflect love, the clouds'
    charactery stars the nothingness.
  The night's pen teems
    with fear. I sink, behold famous
books, magic and alone. I relish
    power, rich grain of hours

never lived. I think and think,
my brain never feeling, never garnering—
Fair creature, look!

I Saw You

James B. Nicola

I saw you last night on the Avenue.
You didn't notice me but I saw you,
looking perfect and dapper in your walk.
You gave me, with your sureness, half a shock
as you approached. I turned to face the glass
of a store display, waiting for you to pass.
In concert with the night, you lingered there
and glanced in the same glass to adjust your hair—
it was only a wisp, a fallen lock
you tucked back. How the light became you then!
I saw your crystal cold reflection
breathe half the night in, on the verge of talking, then walk on. And once more I was free.
I'm pretty sure you didn't notice me.

The Redwood Croft

Teresa Lane

Love is a motel,
people come and go and
leave dirty towels and
take your tiny soaps and shampoos.

There are only occupants,
rarely residents, and yes,
they'll leave, but at least
that is something you can always count on.

Here's another:
there will always be someone to
hold your hand and when there is not,
I will be there.

And a third:
Where ever is your motel,
keep the door unlocked.
I'll sneak in and make a pot of tea,
just how you like,
and leave when you close your eyes.

Under the Sun

I'm in love with love but I ain't in love with no one.
I love the hollyhock and the bees,
sunshine through cottonwood trees but don't love no boy.
Don't love no one but myself, the few I grew up with
and even fewer that I've kept.

The couple of simple things the world does every day,
breezes, warm trickles of rain,
and the grey sliver of moon saying goodbye.
I couldn't love, couldn't love you, couldn't love anything but
lightning bugs and snapdragons and the
chalk chalk pyramids from my childhood.

Boys weren't meant for loving,
they were meant for building and hunting and
I can do all that on my own.
Boys were meant for nothing but rough work and
now that I'm older and grown, I can do just as much.

I don't need no boy, don't need no man,
don't need no one to love but the flare, the shine,
and to bask under the brightest star.

The Little Freak Show

John Randolph Carter

I lather up and follow my shadow.
"The night is young," say the feather dusters.
I polish brass till the cows come home.
(Moo is not a word.)

The savage sentries laugh at my lips.
I pucker and pant and blow them a kiss.
They part company.
I pass through unannounced.

In the theater the cerebral players are gesticulating.
I suffer pangs of doubt and self-pity.
I run out onto the stage and arch.
This causes a commotion in the balcony.

The thrill is back.
I circle the theater three times
then buy a paper and read the reviews.
"He Was Scintillating!"

unrequited

Erica Woiwode Mason

between the whisper
of friendly salutations
and the rush of blood
to the head,
do you know
do you know
    the
        longing
to place your
poems so
ceremoniously
in a circle
around my bed,
and fall asleep
in the middle?
dreaming of
inconsistencies
and illicit
betrayals, the
race to catch
up with what

is far too late
never ending—

the song that
would be my
declaration to
you pulses in
my bloodlines,
as if i could
touch your face
and you would
know all meaning
found in that
purest silence—

as if i could—

in the middle of
the night, i
cradle the image
of you in my
living room,
book in your
hands, your eyes
shifting over
to me every
few lines,
asking questions

telling secrets
without words
as i pretend
not to notice,
my heart telling
you the whole
time just how
        lovely
                you
                        are.

greenwall

Soul surfers,
she calls them,
as if the term
invokes transcendence
into her own
religion—

i watch her
manipulate
the board
as if she has known
all her life
her purpose
to be in the ocean,
follow the tide,
inhale salt-air as
if it were all
that was left
of human decency—

she fights like lions
against capitalist rage,

dreams of politicians
being washed out to sea—

cries softly
at chaos stirring
a monsoon
in her head,
beach empty
at night,
except for this
soul surfer
in the van's
wood-frame bed
that squeaks when
she turns
to listen outside
to the familiar sound
she has set her pulse to—

the sympathetic whisper of ocean.

Little Horses

Betty Moffett

"You'll be so good at this, Honey," Miss Lynn assured her. "I can always count on more-a from Cora."

Cora winced but then put on a smile for her riding teacher. For almost all of her thirteen years, she'd hated her name, though she'd adored her grandmother, the small, sweet and salty woman she'd been named for. Surely, her parents could have anticipated the nicknames other kids would make from "Cora"—Apple Cora, Dora the Explora, and more recently, inevitably, and inaccurately, Cora the hor-a. And now Miss Lynn had joined the fun.

It didn't help that on this blue-bird Saturday morning, while other girls—girls with names like Riley and Kiley—were practicing on the muscled quarter horses for the spring show at Heartland Ranch, she and Miss Lynn were taking three miniature horses to a nursing home. In spite of her mood, Cora grinned. It sounded like the little horses were about to become residents. Then she remembered what her teacher had told her the week before: "Honey," and Cora knew from the "honey" that the news would not be good. "Cora, Honey," Miss Lynn said, "you're just not quite strong enough yet to control those big old quarter horses, but you're a natural with the minis, and guess what we've been asked to do? Take three of those little sweethearts to the nursing home as therapy horses!"

The minis. They were too small to ride and too big to hold on your lap. Cora liked them okay but considered them little freaks, with their tiny, perfect bodies and their thick manes and tails. "Well, maybe I'm a little freak, too," she thought. "Maybe we belong together." She realized that she was indulging in what her grandmother had called "dark drama," a turn of mind she had in fact inherited, along with her small frame, from the elder Cora. Miss Lynn had explained how they'd load three minis—Cora could pick which ones—and take them to Oakland Manor so the residents could see them. They'd be like therapy dogs, only they'd be horses, and "Just think," Miss Lynn told Cora, "how happy you'll be making those old folks." Cora had had some experience with how happy "old folks" were in nursing homes, but she had nodded and tried to look perky.

"Little freaks," Cora thought, as she brushed out John Deere's heavy tail. "Little freaks," she murmured pleasantly to the cluster of yard-high horses who pushed against her, looking for a few oats or a slice of apple. She stopped to consider the minis, to acknowledge their tiny hooves and big eyes, their even, un-pony-like tempers. She felt sorry for the ones she hadn't chosen to go to the nursing home. But Coffee was the steadiest, John Deere, the best looking, and Lilly— well, blonde Lilly was her favorite.

"Never mind," she said to the others, as she slipped three halters on three docile heads. "There won't be any trophies or ribbons. We're just going to see a bunch of old folks, a bunch of old discards." The harsh word was one her grandmother had used to describe herself. "Freaks and Discards," Cora thought. "Sounds like a rock group."

About 10:00, Miss Kim hitched up the rusty stock trailer she used for the minis. "Lead Coffee in first, and the others will come right behind," she said, and then added, "You really are good with them, Cora, Honey." Cora wished her teacher would stop trying to make her feel good. As sure as night follows day, John Deere and Lilly followed their leader into the trailer. And just as surely, three tiny horses made three tiny manure piles on the trailer floor.

"Little pooping freaks," Cora crooned, scratching Lilly under her forelock. She wielded the shovel, then latched the trailer door and climbed into the truck beside her teacher. The low, gray sky promised rain. "Figures," thought Cora.

"Have you been to a nursing home before?" Miss Kim asked, and Cora nodded "yes," remembering Sunday visits to her grandmother. Assuming a cheerfulness none of them felt, she and her mom and dad had driven the thirty-five miles to an Alzheimer's unit in the next town to witness the gradual vanishing of that once-lively lady's memory and wry wit. Before she died, she had forgotten her name. Cora wished she couldn't remember the smells, the sounds, the rounded backs and twisted fingers. "There are places I've liked better," she said, and then smiled to make a small joke out of the truth.

In a very few minutes, they pulled up in the parking lot behind Oakland Manor. Already, an audience had gathered, some in wheelchairs, some with walkers or canes, and Cora felt the same struggle between repulsion and sympathy she'd felt when visiting her grandmother. "Shape up," she told herself, "it's not catching." But she tried not to look at a dignified old woman who was wearing a bib.

Cora heard a soft chorus of "ohhh's" as she led Coffee out, Miss Lynn right behind with John Deere and Lilly. "Wish I could hitch her to a cart and drive out to my farm," a stooped man said, shuffling closer to the horses. "They're precious," said a woman with thin hair, "just look at those eyelashes."

"Well, wouldn't you know," a thin man in a cowboy shirt announced, holding out his hand and squinting at the sky. And sure enough, it had started to drizzle. A couple of women covered their

hair-do's with their hands, but all seemed reluctant to leave the horses. Then, Leo Vetter, the short, tanned administrator of the Manor,
straightened his tie and said, "What the heck. Bring 'em inside. We've
cleaned up bigger messes than these ponies can make." And Cora
and Miss Lynn led their charges into the spacious social center. Right
away, the audience increased, some on wheels, some supported by
aides who spoke encouragingly into old ears, "Yes, they're real. Yes,
you can touch them."

Cora noticed hands that shook and heads that bobbed uncontrollably; she caught a subtle version of the powdery smell she remembered from her grandmother's room. But she also saw smiles and heard
murmurs of delight, and she realized that not all of the compliments
were for the horses. "What a cute little figure the girl has," she heard
one woman say to another, and since Miss Lynn was neither girl nor
little, Cora understood they were taking about her. One woman who
had rolled her wheel chair as close as possible to John Deere touched
Cora's arm and said, "We don't get to see many pretty young people.
You're sweet to come."

Warmed by such appreciation and encouraged by the horses'
good behavior, Cora began to relax. Then someone said, "What about
Thelma?" and someone else said, "Bless her heart, she always did love
horses, but you know she can't come out here. Her knees are so bad
and she has—what's that word? Demanded? Deminted?" Leo Vetter
looked thoughtful and then held a quick conference with the aides. To
Cora, he said, "Can you take just one of them down the hall to room
132?" Cora took Lilly's lead from Miss Kim and said, "Yes, I can."

Right away, she was sorry. She had a pretty good idea of what
she'd find in room 132: someone even more disabled than the wrinkled
crowd surrounding the horses; someone confused and clutching, like

the woman her grandmother had become. As Lilly's hooves clicked down the hallway, the light became dimmer and the familiar sweetish smell increased. By the time Cora found the right room, she was taking shallow breaths and her heart was making her shirt flutter. The door was open. "Miss Thelma?" she said to the figure in a huge padded chair. Thelma's broad, pale face had no expression. She was saying something that sounded like "Totem toe," and there were bubbles on her lips. And then she saw Lilly. "Oh my, is this a dream? I think I see a little horse and a girl angel. Please, can you get that pony over here where I can put my hand on it?" Cora led Lilly forward until her nose touched the arm of the big chair. Thelma's swollen fingers reached out and found the spot under Lilly's forelock that Cora always scratched. "I was saying the multiplication tables when you came in," Thelma confided. "I can still get through the 2's." And then, "A lot of them don't like folks messing with their ears, do they, but I could tell this one wouldn't mind. How many hands tall is she? She's shaped too good to be a pony."

"She's just under eight hands," Cora said, "and you're right, she's not a pony, she's a miniature horse.

"Oh good, you talked and you made sense, so this must not be a dream. I've dreamed horses before, you know." Thelma's face had changed; her eyes were clear and her cheeks were a faint pink. With her hand resting on Lilly's neck, she began to tell Cora about a horse called Slicker. "She was a spoiled little beast with one lucky white foot, and I was the only one who could ride her. She didn't like boys—threw them off." Thelma's laugh had a click in it. Then she looked up at Cora. "Say, you're not a relative, are you? Sometimes they come and say' Cousin Thelma' and 'Aunt Thelma,' and I have no idea. Did you tell me your name was Nancy, angel girl?"

"Well, no. It's Cora.'

Thelma held out her hand to Cora, who hesitated before taking it.

"Cora's a good name. I bet I can remember that one. And you're a real girl, not an angel. I got that right, didn't I?

"I'm real," said Cora, smiling at Thelma.

Then Lilly stamped her foot and snorted, twice. "I'd better get her out of here, or we're going to have—a mess," Cora said. But Thelma's grip tightened on her hand and she said, "Oh, please don't go."

A little thrill of panic hit Cora's stomach as she remembered her grandmother holding on to her parents, pleading to be taken home. Then Thelma took a deep breath and let go Cora's hand. "It's just for two minutes. I want to call my daughter and tell her about this. But if I say I've got a horse in my room…well, you see the problem, Carol?"

So Cora scratched Lilly's belly and waited while Thelma slowly pushed the big numbers on her telephone.

"Debby, I've got…" she began, and then passed the phone to Cora. "You tell her."

"Your mother's fine," Cora said, "and she wants you to know she has a beautiful little horse in her room, a real one, right beside her chair."

Thelma held out her hand for the phone and blew a kiss as Cora led Lilly from the room. Thelma was telling her daughter, "Rose or Violet or something like that. No, that's the horse's name, silly. The girl's name is Cora."

Letter in Praise of Fairy Tale

Andrea Scarpino

Dear girl too-beautiful, boy

lost-in-the-woods. Dear hunter.

Dear heart-cut-from. Dear ache.

Dear human flesh, poison-swig.

Dear tower, witch, fiery breath.

Wolf, fox, snake, talking fish.

Dear riddle. Promises: child,

marriage bed, kingdom, riches.

Dear kiss. Dear shifting shape.

Dear mother-missing, coffin lid.

Dear trickery, wit. Death, bested.

Winter, Stalingrad, 1942–43

Stanley Morris Noah

There was a battle here. The
mighty 6th German army fought
Russian armies for seven months.
After the thing was over, one
million men were killed. How do
you tell a story, a battle without

using the word, blood. I'll try.
I can only say, soldiers were fed
into the carnage with little regard
for their lives. Each side sensed
who ever won this battle shall win
the war. Fighting got so hot during

falling snow flakes that dogs swam
across the Don River just to get away
from the burning noise of death. The
frozen dead looked like mannequins
on white cloth landscapes. Some
stacked in piles like rotten fruit. When

it was over in a city of 50,000, only
1,500 citizens emerged slowly from
underground. Years passed. A soldier's
letter written in pencil was found, saying,

"Can't get out. Remember me, goodbye.
Tell the children I love them."

Water Cycle

Lisa Ohlen Harris

January in Oregon

Wind blows the rain against my windows and in it I see chunks of hail, melting as they slide down the glass. My front lawn and garden are a series of small lakes; the backyard is a slope of mud reaching all the way to the rising creek. It has been raining for two weeks without a break: the ground is sodden. Even though it's the dead of winter, everything is green. Rocks and rooftops and even the bare branches of the oaks across the creek are velveted with moss.

My children learn the water cycle—evaporation, condensation, precipitation—as I learned when I was very small. We know that this water is not new: this rain has been around since the time of Noah, since long-necked dinosaurs swam in the floodwaters.

February in Mongolia

When the U.S. Ambassador leaves Ulaanbaatar to go on vacation, he and his wife sleep in a yurt. I know this because my friend Jonathan is the U.S. Ambassador to Mongolia, and in this coldest month, he and Fiona have traveled to the Lake Hovsgol Ice Festival. The lake is completely frozen over—two feet thick in most places, its appearance alternating cloudy and clear. The ice is deep blue, spiderwebbed with cracks. Gazing at Jonathan's photos is like meditating on a batik—like looking up into a clouded and crazed sky. A yak kneels to drink from a hole bored in the lake. Mongolian children clamber for position atop a slide carved of ice: their eyes peek out from a rainbow of quilted and padded and fur-lined garments, knit scarves wrapped and tied over chins and mouths and noses.

Adults in traditional dress gather on the lake to choose sides and stretch a long rope for the annual massive tug of war. Afterwards, the women will arm wrestle on ice slabs, while the young men lace up ice skates for the big race.

A boy rides an ice-sculpted lake monster. The creature's clear dorsal fins sparkle like crystal, magnifying the blue of the sky and the forest green of the boy's coat. His mittened hands grasp the glassy forefin and he looks back over his shoulder, as if being pursued. The ambassador holds his camera steady and freezes the moment.

March in Scandinavia

In Scandinavia, the land of my ancestors, musician Terje Isungset plays concerts in ice caverns on instruments carved from ancient glaciers. He performs wearing a thick parka and a fur hat with earflaps and long braided tassels. His eyes come alive as he pulls off heavy gloves to tap ice chimes with his bare fingers. The colder it is, the more resonant the tones. "I have to listen to my instrument," Isungset says. "Instead of [me] deciding how it's going to sound, the instrument decides how I will play it."

He carves an ice horn from pure glacier ice thousands of years old. Each time he lifts the horn to his lips, part of the instrument melts away.

April in Oregon

I arrive at The Coffee Cottage a little after eight, but the music hasn't started yet. I unzip my raincoat and pull off my gloves. "Okay if I sit with you?" Marj nods.

Her eighteen-year-old daughter, Consuela, plunks a note on the old black upright piano and tunes her guitar. Soon Consuela strums a chord and begins to sing her mother's lilting version of a Van Morrison song. Marj harmonizes from our adjacent table as she reaches into her tote bag. Nearby a small girl in hot pink leggings blows on her cocoa. Two college students carry their drinks and laptop to the back corner, as far from the music as they can get.

"These nights are hard," Marj whispers, "because people aren't always here for the music."

Marj has been performing since she was Consuela's age as part of the '60s Jesus Movement in Southern California. Her forty-year-old record albums are propped on the piano: on one, Marj walks the beach in moccasins, carrying her guitar over her shoulder; on another album she stands against a forest backdrop, surrounded by wildflowers.

Marj picks up her guitar, takes Consuela's place, and plays the music I've loved my entire life: Joni Mitchell, Bruce Cockburn, and James Taylor. "Play 'Chelsea Morning,'" someone says, and Marj cranks her guitar into one of Joni's alternate tunings: Marj sings it her own way, though, and the song becomes hers. I'm watching a middle aged woman with wire-rimmed glasses and a flowing scarf over her tunic, but when I close my eyes I see the seventeen-year-old Jesus Freak who's been born again and cut her first album.

Steam from hot drinks and our breathing and singing rises and condenses on the inside of the windows. The girl in pink leggings extends her forefinger and draws a wobbly smiley face.

May in Mongolia
It is late spring in Mongolia, and I am thinking of the boy from the ice festival. Surely by now he has shed his mittens and padded coat. I see

him riding bareback on a stocky, long-tailed Mongolian horse across steppes scattered with wildflowers, stopping under batik skies to draw up the water skin strapped to his belt. He tips his head back and takes a long draught of water.

June in Oregon

We set down our water bottles at the end of the rows and begin to pick—and eat. We've come with empty bellies and buckets to fill with the first berries of the season. In July we will pick faster and put more of the berries into our buckets and fewer into our mouths. By the end of August, we will have forty pounds of frozen raspberries, blueberries, and blackberries.

I wipe my hands on my jeans and take from my pocket a small camera. My daughter Ashley is intent on picking blueberries, her favorite. Ashley's body frames the right side of the photograph, arm extended to the bush, lips pursed in concentration. A few rows behind Ashley, my mother is picking blueberries, too, a nice visual echo for the photograph. It is not until hours later, after we've returned from the fields and spread the berries on cookie sheets to freeze, that I look at the photos and see what I missed in the berry fields. My mother's lips are pursed in the same expression as her granddaughter's. She seems to be a smaller reflection of my daughter, and I imagine my own grandmother superimposed in the distance behind my mother, like those endless images in an angled department store mirror, going back, back, back.

July in Scandinavia

Grandpa Emil would tell me about summertime in Sweden, the days so long and bright that the sun would barely set before it rose again.

His eyes shone with that remembered light, so bright that I longed for Scandinavia, too. Before Grandpa died, he showed me the veins on the inside of my arms, blue beneath my skin. He told me I carried the blue blood of the Vikings, that we Ohlens were descended from Erik the Red. Now the Ohlen grandchildren and great-grandchildren are spread across the Pacific Northwest, where summer evenings are long and light.

August in Mongolia

Mongolia's northern border arcs and scallops like a tulip opening to meet south central Russia and is cupped by the People's Republic of China to the west, south, and east. There are no fences out on the steppes, only wildflowers and grass in a great circle as far as the eye can see. Ride a horse away from your grandfather's yurt until all the world is a vast bowl and you and your horse stand in the middle of land and sky.

At night you and your father and grandfathers will sleep in the family yurt with a circle of stars all around: a bowl within a bowl.

September in Oregon

I heap a large roasting pan with frozen berries, mixing in sugar, whole wheat pastry flour to thicken, and a bit of water to create some extra juice. The result will be a thick chunky syrup to mix into plain yogurt or dollop over waffles or ice cream. The juice of these berries is the rain of last spring and as the compote bakes I look out my kitchen window where bright clouds stretch and shift across the sky.

An hour later my house smells delicious and I lift the roasting pan out onto the stovetop to cool. The steam is thick and sweet and when I breathe through my mouth, I sense tartness on the side of my tongue. When the berries have cooled enough, I eat spoonful after spoonful. I taste summer. I swallow last spring's rain.

October in Oregon

The autumn winds have peeled off so many maple leaves that our sidewalk is a rainbow of red, orange, and gold. Just as I'm thinking about what to fix for dinner, I look out the front window to see kids from the neighborhood raking my front yard. Up and down the street for three houses are rakes and brooms and children and adults, too: I grab my camera and step outside.

The children pile leaves as high as the smallest child among them: they leap and toss and re-gather and fling their laughter into the dimming afternoon. One boy jumps into the wheelbarrow and my daughter grabs the handles and hurtles wagon and boy down the street. The children hoist themselves up into the maples, seeing who can climb highest. I stand with the setting sun to my back and take photo after photo, before the light fails entirely.

Every October there's a day like this. On some unscheduled afternoon, the children seem to just know. Do they sense the change in the air? Because this ritual marks a change: the rains will become more steady after this day, and the children will move their play indoors.

As I snap pictures, five neighbor ladies keep a watchful eye on the children, moving the rakes to safety as wagons and wheelbarrows clatter down the sidewalk. I glance behind me to see one woman take another into her arms. For what loss, what pain, I don't know.

But here is what I do know. Among these mothers and these children still lives the memory of a baby girl. Though I never knew her, when I snap a photo of her brother and sister in the leaves, I see her dimples in their cheeks, her bright eyes in theirs.

November in Scandinavia

My first child was born a week before I turned thirty-one. I myself was born on Armistice Day, 1963: eleventh day, eleventh month—and eleven days before Kennedy's assassination. Grandpa Emil was born in November, too, more than a century ago and a half a world away.

It snowed in Nedansjö the day Grandpa Emil was born. The older children gathered clean snow into a pot and brought it to their grandmother, who melted it over the fire for *fruktsoppa*. She soaked the dried fruit then added a cinnamon stick and some sugar—last of all a fresh apple fetched from the cellar. She left the steaming pot to cool while she kneaded three pinches of ground cardamom into her bread dough. Later she would bring a dish of the thick, sweet soup and a pungent slice of fresh bread to strengthen the nursing mother.

Evaporation, condensation, precipitation. Emil would cross the ocean, take a wife, build a life in America. Four children. A business. A home built by his own hands. A boat to ride the waves of the Puget Sound. Blue-blooded grandchildren eating Grandma's thin Swedish pancakes with tart jelly from the Old Country and asking for more.

December in Oregon

Rain falls, tapping the skylight, glossing the deck, clinging to the bare aspen branches outside my kitchen window. Our Christmas tree is decorated with straw ornaments from the Old Country: hearts and stars and *julbocken*, along with handpainted *dala* horses from Auntie Ingeborg. It's a live tree this year—a Noble Fir, exactly Ashley's height—and after Christmas we will pull on rubber boots and dig a wide hole to plant the tree down by the creek. After we've tamped the soil down all around, I will freeze the moment in a photograph of Ashley next to the newly planted tree. I will tell my grandchildren that the tall fir by the creek used to be the same height as Aunt Ashley. I will tell them they are descended from Vikings, that their blood is blue.

Christmas lights wink. My bread machine hums. There's snow in the forecast.

But Light is Nothing

Paul Nelson

We began by thinking our shadows
kept us vague and lovely in each other's eyes.
This we could live with on the forest floor
where sunlight pecks like gold, feral chickens
in leafmeal shade.

Later, we watched them on the sidewalk,
the tarmac and barbered lawns,
saw them guess at stairs, rails, barely
getting along, knew the slow
cloaks lengthening, swelling,
shrinking and receding.
We understood the deadly sun,

squint at these flayed, dark,
romantic reputations the children come to visit
then flee, fly off to see their own shrouds
like burkas on desert places.

Diving, masked, wearing tanks of ecstasy,
air from their world frees them
to fin down, lay exotic mantas on the soaked

dust of the sea's floor. Young, they can be startled
by what swims along so easily below them.

Like us they glance up to quivering light
(nothing in and of itself) relieved
by emanation that casts us all
because we fear to find
just ourselves.

Dear Editor

Lee Rossi

Occasionally I dream about those Chilean miners trapped half a mile underground with little food and water, with nothing in fact but time to tell and re-tell their stories to one another in the dark, and I wonder how different they are from writers, who elaborate and polish their stories until finally they are rescued from the tedium of revision by a merciful editor. Or are they a figure for the editors themselves, living in forced seclusion during their yearly/semi-annual/or quarterly reading period? Is the slush pile any less daunting than seven hundred meters of rock? The fact is, even after our escape, none of us is liable to receive a $200 pair of sunglasses. We'll have to face the glare of our situation without anything to buffer its impact.

Be that as it may I'm hoping that you'll let the enclosed poem free us from our respective prisons.

Horizon Event

That winter I wore two sweaters
and an extra roll of fat,
the life belt that kept me afloat
in a featureless, sucking ocean.

Up the horizon came the reggae
of party ships. "Read this," friends
called from the brightly colored decks,
brightly colored books chunking divots

from my scalp and shoulders.
Self-loathing, self-love,
I was capable of neither.
A new scripture was being written

and a new Jerusalem peopled
with the happily, self-satisfied.
I wanted to shout,
"I deserve to suffer,"

who had never known anything
but self-inflicted pain.

Nemesis, that friendly goddess
came dressed like a distant relative

holding store-bought flowers
as for a hospital visit.
We danced, I was on deck now,
a tenement deflecting the wrecking

ball's insistent hand.
And yet I wanted to collapse,
a pile of rubble
secret as a tomb.

The angel laughed, the dark
goddess brighter now
than morning, and dragged me
from my bed. "Look at that,"

she whispered, lovers
touching hands and hair.
"They do not deserve this
happiness, but it is theirs."

When Jesus invited the cripple to
carry the burden of his stretcher,
how long was he grateful?
I'll bet it was hot in Palestine

and the crowd of well-wishers
had run off after Jesus,
hungry for the next magic show.
And what about the bearers,

suddenly unemployed?
Or poor dead Lazarus
stepping from the cool of his crypt
into the glare of public regard?

Did he ever wash the stench
from his raddled skin
or comprehend his sister's sadness
at her sudden loss of freedom?

It's been three years since you left
and still my nerves are tangled
in the body's wiring cabinet,
neurons firing like accidental cannons

in autonomic night. I am saved,
cast on shore with the other refugees
from love. No surprise that some of us
swim past the reef and lose ourselves in the depths.

Every so often I look to the horizon
and notice a cloud sailing like a comma
at the edge of sight.
Is that your ship? Returning?

Coffin

Rachel Squires Bloom

In the train station,
one black-clad knee pointed
toward me the other toward
the platform where trains nestle
in then push out, you describe
the casket you have bought your mother,
its high polish and fine design a spit
in death's bleak, unavoidable face.

Your gold-spoked eyes shine
in the delight that even your clean-freak
mom would take in this wooden box;
not even her Judgment Day could urge
her to rise and buff it to high shine.
Its luster would exceed all expectations,
the one last act of love you can give
the old woman, love or hate her but bless
her heart and despite the fact
that you will hold the knowing
for you both.

As If It Never Happened

Tanque R. Jones

They know but they won't tell me,
say it's best I don't know whether it's a boy or girl. I think boy,
though I would want a girl.

The machine vrooms awake. Every scrape of the wand makes
him disappear. A nurse sorts through pieces, checks for major
parts, counts arms, legs, fingers, toes. "I can't find the..."

some medical term I've never heard. The beast roars again,
hunts for last bits of baby. "Oh, there it is. Never mind."

They warn, "You might see pieces of tissue that look like bits of
liver." I pee, bathe in darkness, terrified I might see some
reminder of him.

Momma says now I can get on with my life.

The Ripple Effect

Kristen Svenson

Read through, then read in reverse order, paragraph by paragraph.

Carlos sits on the side of the road.

His hands clasp. His head hangs. A small puddle grows.

A crowd gathers. The people distant.

The blood drains from his face.

A tiny flutter beats.

Carlos is alone.

Carlos sits on the side of the road.

His sister huddles next to him.

The wind blows fiercely between them.

His hands clasp. His head hangs. A small puddle grows.

He can feel her body tremble against his side. He can see the colors making love.

A crowd gathers before him. The people seem so distant.

The blood drains from his face.

A tiny flutter beats.

Carlos is alone.

Carlos sits on the side of the road.

His sister huddles next to him. Her name is Esther.

The wind blows fiercely between them, a faint ringing of piercing quality.

His hands clasp in fists. His head hangs between his knees. A small puddle grows between his feet.

Esther's shaking sobs do not reach him, but he can feel her body tremble against his side. Carlos cannot bring himself to look up. He can see the colors making love.

A crowd gathers before him. The people seem so distant, even Esther. He steals a glance at her face.

His arms surround his head. The blood drains from his face.

A tiny flutter beats beneath his chest.

Carlos is alone.

Carlos sits on the side of the road.

His sister huddles next to him, shivering as goosebumps spread beneath her clothing. Her name is Esther.

The wind blows fiercely between them, a faint ringing of piercing quality in his ears that resounds and throbs.

His hands clasp in fists until his nails break the surface. His head hangs between his knees, pounding with a million thoughts. A small puddle grows larger between his feet.

Esther's shaking sobs do not reach him, but he can feel her body tremble against his side as she clutches at his shirt. She jerks his arm, but Carlos cannot bring himself to look up. He can see the colors making love in the watery pool. A salty mixture.

A crowd gathers before him, as he knew it would. The people seem so distant, even Esther. He steals a glance at her face.

The silence around him is frightening. His arms surround his head. The blood drains from his face.

A tiny flutter beats beneath his chest.

Carlos is alone.

Carlos sits on the side of the road.

His sister huddles next to him, shivering as goosebumps spread beneath her clothing—a soft summer dress and leather jacket that should be keeping her warm. Her name is Esther.

The wind blows fiercely between them, a faint ringing of piercing quality in his ears that resounds and throbs. They all have different meanings.

Carlos ignores the sting. His hands clasp in fists until his nails break the surface. His head hangs between his knees, pounding with a million thoughts. A small puddle grows larger between his feet. It shouldn't be that color.

Esther's shaking sobs, which grow in power and intensity, do not reach him, but he can feel her body tremble against his side as she clutches at his shirt. Her struggle is fascinating, but it horrifies Carlos just the same. She jerks his arm, but Carlos cannot bring himself to look up, focusing instead on that growing puddle—wondering. He can see the colors making love in the watery pool. A salty mixture.

A crowd gathers before him, as he knew it would when he helped Esther stumble to the side of the road. The people seem so distant, even Esther, who still sits beside him. He steals a glance at her face, desperately trying to soothe her.

The silence around him is frightening because he knows that it is not real. His arms surround his head in this crouched position. Carlos cannot face what must be before him. The blood drains from his face.

A tiny flutter of life beats like a heartbeat beneath his chest.

The world around him is falling away.

In many ways, Carlos is alone.

Carlos sits on the side of the road, surrounded by broken glass.

His sister huddles next to him, shivering as goosebumps spread beneath her clothing—a soft summer dress and leather jacket that should be keeping her warm. Her name is Esther.

The wind blows fiercely between them, pushing away the uniformed man that towers above in condescending accusation. There is a faint ringing of piercing quality in his ears that resounds and throbs with the essence of remorseful agony. They all have different meanings.

Carlos watches the pain but ignores the sting. His hands clasp in fists until his nails break the surface. His head hangs between his knees, pounding with a million thoughts. A small puddle grows larger between his feet. It shouldn't be that color.

Esther's shaking sobs, which grow in power and intensity with each passing minute, do not reach him, but he can feel her body tremble against his side as she clutches at his shirt. It's already torn, so her perfect nails do not bother him as they rip through the cloth. Her struggle is fascinating, but it horrifies Carlos just the same. She stares in that hollow silence as though she does not really see him, as though she never really has. She jerks his arm, but Carlos cannot bring himself to look up, focusing instead on that growing puddle—wondering. He can see the colors making love in the watery pool. A salty mixture of the tears from his eyes, the pain from his heart, and the blood from his veins that is slowly draining away.

A crowd gathers before him, as he knew it would when he helped Esther stumble to the side of the road to escape the crunch of metal that lies behind them. The people seem so distant, even Esther, who still sits beside him. He steals a glance at her face, desperately trying to soothe her, to make the tears that fall from her eyes disappear.

The remaining silence around him is frightening, because he knows that it is not real. It cannot be real. His arms surround his head as he hunches in this crouched position—shielding himself from the world. Carlos cannot face what must be before him. The blood drains from his face, from his soul.

A tiny flutter of life beats like a heartbeat beneath his chest, a rhythm that races beyond control and grips his throat.

The world around him is falling away. His lips move to form words, but no sound escapes.

In many ways, Carlos is alone.

Carlos sits on the side of the road, staring down at his body, surrounded by broken glass.

His sister huddles next to him, shivering as goosebumps spread beneath her clothing—a soft summer dress and leather jacket that should be keeping her warm. Her name is Esther.

The wind blows fiercely between them, pushing away the uniformed man that towers above in condescending accusation. There is a faint ringing of piercing quality in his ears that resounds and throbs with the essence of remorseful agony. Vehicles shriek their urgency. They all have different meanings.

Carlos watches the pain but ignores the sting. He doesn't even feel it. His hands clasp in fists until his nails break the surface. His head hangs between his knees, pounding with a million thoughts and questions. A small puddle grows larger between his feet. It shouldn't be that color; rain does not resemble the redness of sweet, honeysuckle cherries.

Esther's shaking sobs, which grow in power and intensity with each passing minute, do not reach him, but he can almost feel her body tremble against his side as she clutches at his shirt. It's already torn, so her perfect nails do not bother him as they rip through the cloth. Her struggle is fascinating, but it horrifies Carlos just the same, because the desperation in her eyes does not reflect in those of the body next to her. She stares in that hollow silence as though she does not really see him, as though she never really has. She jerks his arm, but Carlos cannot bring himself to look up, focusing instead on that growing puddle and the ripples of the drops as they fall—wondering what has made them so dark, so beautiful. He can see the colors making love in the watery pool. A salty mixture of the tears from his eyes, the pain from his heart, and the blood from his veins that is slowly draining away. They mock him with their dye.

A crowd gathers before him, as he knew it would when he helped Esther stumble to the side of the road to escape the crunch of metal that lies behind them. The people seem so distant in his mind, even Esther, who still sits beside him. He steals a glance at her face, which seems to move farther and farther away, desperately trying to soothe her, to make the tears that fall from her burnt mahogany eyes disappear.

The remaining silence around him is frightening, because he knows that it is not real. It cannot be real. It sings of denouement. His arms surround his head as he hunches in this crouched position, muscles clenched in steel resilience—shielding himself from the world. Carlos cannot face what must be before him. The blood drains from his face, from his soul, and he wonders if his life has really come to such an ending.

A tiny flutter of life beats like a heartbeat beneath his chest, a rhythm that races beyond control and grips his throat. Carlos cannot tell if the resounding thumps belong to him, or to someone else.

The world around him is evaporating. His lips move to form words, but no sound escapes. The scene slips away, though Carlos is the only one to leave.

In every way, Carlos is alone.

Last Daughter

Dear Mother,

How strange to find myself writing to you after all these years—
no longer a child, in the throes of adolescence, drawing a picture that
will never be delivered to its rightful owner. I have neither updates
of my personal life to give nor dramatic tales to regale in a flurry of
excitement. No, I am writing to you now, of all times, with nothing to
offer you at all. How strange life has turned out to be.

I have had much time to reminisce about those days of naiveté.
To think about the lies I so devotedly believed. To remember how, in
the innocence of childhood, I would slowly and methodically write to
you, every Sunday. How strange it seems now that your silent replies
never swayed me. I was assuaged by the promises that were so often
told, so easily believed, and so frequently broken. Next week, next
month, next year—they all held the same meaning. No matter how
many times they fell through, the promises kept alive the hope that I
was wanted, needed, loved. I would bend over my writing table loy-
ally; knowing, or rather, hoping that your long absences were uninten-
tional. I firmly believed that if you could find a way to contact me you
would. And so I waited.

How asinine it all seems now. Summers turned into summers,
and my toddler sized writing table was replaced with one for a child,
and then a teenager, and then an adult; and still I believed. I never qua-

vered in my devotion to you, mother, which is why I now wonder how you ever could have faltered in your devotion to me.

I remember the world that I lived in back then. It was an auspicious world full of love and opportunity. Daddy saw to our every need. We always had food to eat and warm blankets at night. There were never any monsters under my bed, mother, because Daddy always made sure to get rid of them before I fell asleep. Yet it would be delusive to say that there were never any tears. There were always tears. Sometimes they would arrive in the form of a scraped knee or, later in life, a forsaken beau. There was never anybody to dry those tears, for Daddy did not believe in that kind of infirmity. "C'mon now sweetie, suck it up," was the most affection we'd get for sodden eyes.

I don't blame Daddy for this childhood neglect, for he was a very strong man, irreprehensible in every other aspect. He joined in our games frequently, a wry grin spreading over his coarse, hardened face as we shared in moments of fantasy and intrigue. Those were feelings of contentment that washed over our small childhood dwelling— like distant winds cavorting through the wooden hallways so lovingly adorned with the steady passage of time.

But who to turn to when the absurdities of life were too much to handle? Who to share my innermost thoughts with, my deepest emotions, my girlish aspirations for the future, my fluttering affections for different boys? It was my writing that I had to depend on for this companionship, mother. My writing became my outlet, my solitary confidant, my hidden reprieve. Laurie was much too sophisticated and grown-up to bother with the petty annoyances of a younger sister, and the thought of approaching Daddy with the woes of my tangled love life was frightening. Nevertheless, it was Daddy who prepared us for life as grown women, Mother, but it should have been you. It should have been you.

Women. That is what we are now, Mother, just like you. I wonder which one of us resembles you the most? Laurie's long dark hair with her face full of freckles, just like Daddy's, and her skin resembling the darkest amber? Or my creamy skin and lighter, curlier hair? There are no angel kisses upon my rosy cheeks, and my height is far beneath that of Daddy and Laurie. Auntie Charlotte is always telling me I look exactly like you did at my age, but I hope she's mistaken. I don't think I'm anything like you, Mother. I love my children, and I will never leave them.

Love and loss—they seem to always have been present in our lives. Laurie was the first to experience them, to know the bitter flavor of ardency gone awry. But I soon had my turn as well, Mother, and I learned quickly the lessons that you still don't seem to comprehend. It was through these lessons that I found my Matthew.

Faith is the heart of our affection, the endurance of our marriage: faith in one another, faith in our bond, faith in life itself. We share the love of two separate wholes merged to build one complete vessel of unity; able to float independently, but more majestic when together. Literature has been the outlet of our love, an anchor to ground us in the utopia of our romance, despite the hard times we often struggle with. We would scrutinize the lyrically beautiful poetry of Blake and Yeats alike, affectionately recreating our favorite verses to match our own epic romance. From the adversity and parody of Shakespeare, to the snarky audacity of Dickens, we've shared a connection within the written world that has only been matched by our affinity toward one another in real life. I know you would love him, Mother, if you were around to know him.

But happiness is a fickle friend, Mother, only briefly held by some, and not at all by others. It never arrived for Laurie—sweet and sensitive Laurie, lost in a world of unpredictability. To please, she was always trying to please. Daddy never saw it, Mother, but she was always like that, ever so secretly. It consumed her life and overpowered her brain. A less than perfect grade became a reason to punish herself. A broken romance became a tragedy of unparalleled heights. She was caught in a web of attempted perfection that was always dangling just beyond her grasp.

As we grew older it was still there, hidden beneath the surface of her perfect facade.

When Matthew and I made the announcement about our engagement I saw the glint of panic behind her eyes. How could I, the youngest, marry before her? Yes, Mother, I saw it, but I ignored it. It was a childhood problem, an illness that must be overcome for Laurie to actually live her life. I did not believe I could help her, and I knew she would not accept my help if it was offered. Thus, I remained silent, Mother, and Laurie never hinted at her jealousy.

Soon Matthew and I were celebrating the birth of our little girl. Matthew argued with me for months over the name, but I would not budge in my decision. She was christened Laurie Ann Edwards— a token to my childhood affection for my sister. I wanted to show Laurie how perfect she was in my eyes; how I cherished her so much that I would name my first born in her honor. Laurie didn't see it as such, however. To her, little Laurie was an insult, a knife in the gut of her life-long attempt at perfection. A child is a token of pride and achievement, something to be celebrated, but also something Laurie did not possess. The perfect baby girl I presented to the new and hesitant aunt was a threat to Laurie's livelihood. She could not stand to look at her.

It was then that she started to pull away.

You could have helped her, Mother. You could have shown her that all was not lost in her attempt to live the perfect life. Why weren't you here to protect your girls? Surly you knew the destruction that would soon arrive in place of your absence! For destruction indeed came. I shall always remember the last phone call Laurie offered me, her final attempt to find some perfection in her seemingly forsaken life.

It was a Tuesday. It was raining. Matthew set his morning mug of coffee on the counter and left for work, kissing little Laurie and me on his way out the door. My little girl was only two years old then. We hadn't heard from Laurie in several months but, by that time, the silence was to be expected. I had no idea how to bridge the gap between my sister and me, so I respected the calamity and did not interfere with her soul search.

The telephone rang a little after eight. I know because I was still washing the dishes from the morning meal in the kitchen, little Laurie playing with her doll at my feet. I dried my hands on the apron across my waist and picked up the receiver before the third ring. My heart jumped when I heard Laurie's voice come over the line.

Silence overpowered much of the conversation, and the crinkle in my forehead deepened as her desperation became apparent. We talked about life and the upcoming holiday season.

I asked her to visit for Christmas.

She said she couldn't make it.

I asked about her work at the bakery.

She told me she had quit.

I asked how she was doing.

She said she had to go.

As I hung-up the telephone, my first warning was my racing heart, which beat like the wings of a hummingbird beneath my ruffled blouse. Yet nothing concerned me more than the mournful whimpering of little Laurie a few minutes later, running to me and wrapping her arms around my legs as if hiding from a monster. I phoned Matthew immediately and, within the hour, both he and Daddy were at the house and I was delineating the strangeness of the phone call. We were all huddled in the sitting room, the rain still pouring down the windowpane, when the phone rang once more. This time, Matthew answered it.

The look of fear and sadness that drenched his mottled green eyes as he responded to the person on the other line, the worried glances he shot me as he answered some routine questions—regret, grief, horror—I shall never forget them as long as I live.

What would you have done, Mother, receiving that phone call from your self-ostracized daughter? Would you have rushed to find her? Would you have tried harder to keep her talking?

No, Mother, you would not. You would not have even answered the phone. You would not have been there to hear it ring.

We all mourned. We mourned for Laurie and the unexpected finality of her unfulfilled life. We mourned for the moments we all remembered; for those joyous experiences of childhood; for the present times of sorrow; for hardship, delight, and love. These were the things that had been cruelly altered in the mind of my sister, twisted into a shape that was impossible for her to wrap her heart around. She did not see the beauty in her existence, so she tossed it aside in a swift act of melancholia.

Oh Laurie, sweet Laurie of my childhood. You never deserved the tragedies that were doomed to befall you.

As the days passed by, beyond that first fateful morning, I could do nothing but stare at the yawning hole that manifested itself in my heart and within my home. For weeks I blamed myself. How could I not have known? My own sister...

Thanks to Daddy, and a great deal of support from Matthew, I slowly began to see the truth in the matter. In many ways, Laurie was right. We both lacked something in our lives, something that would always keep us from being perfectly whole. Can you guess what that something was, Mother? I'm sure you can.

My sister's desperation had been growing for years, burrowing itself in the dregs of her unfulfilled brain. This was not just a simple act of retribution by a sad, lonely woman. No. Her defiance began breeding long ago, itching to escape since the abandonment of childhood. You may wonder, Mother, am I angry? Looking back upon the years of misconstrued neglect, finally understanding the deeper meaning behind them, am I tortured by the knowledge? Have the lies that were told, the web of lies that has now finally caught its prey, become a figment of vexation and revenge?

No, Mother. I am not angry.

I am not like you.

Mother, you must have known the evil misconceptions that were bound to stir beneath the surface of your eldest daughter! Do you begin to see the pieces falling into place? The world she created, piece by miserable piece, building up to the destructive finale? How could you not? You are the one that created them.

It has been Matthew that has kept me sane through it all, Mother. I told you how wonderful he is. His beautiful green eyes, like the shoreline—they shield me from the rifts and breaks, shroud my sadness in a torrent of endless companionship. His voice that first night after Laurie's death was healing, soothing the fire within my soul as we recited, in unison, Blake's "Broken Love." A momentary feeling of serenity enveloped me then, but even the safety of my husband's arms cannot protect me from the fearful symmetry of my dreams.

For I have been dreaming of her, Mother, every night. She comes into my room, a look of triumph on her face, having finally achieved the only perfection she could. Do you know what she does, Mother, as she enters my dreams at night?

She laughs at me.

It echoes through my brain, the hunter in the final act of victory. She looks at me, and I know that she feels she has won at last. Then she is gone, vanished, before I can make her face all the cruelty she has wrought.

How strange life has turned out to be after all, Mother. You were never around to fix the damage you created in your daughters, and look at what has become of it! You might deny it.

You might say it was not your fault. But I know the truth, Mother. I know the truth. And I shall never, ever, forget it.

Lovingly,

Your Last Daughter

Journey for Truth

Dylan Dean Plotner

As we search, the world grows much larger with every step taken.
Because it is so big, it's easy to lose our way.
Becoming lost even within ourselves.
Why we continue is a riddle that is left with no answers, or many.
We are not gifted with the knowledge of what lies ahead.
Yet we are driven toward the future.
We could continue to the end and not find the answers we seek.
For time is the only truth.

The Shoetree

Jack e Lorts

Highway 97
snakes its way
through fields
of juniper
and sagebrush,
sweeps across
Juniper Butte—
and there it stands:
the Shoetree,
hung like a
silver saddle
in mourning,
adorned like
the limbs of a
lonely skeleton,
perched atop
a solitary knoll,
Christ-like,
limbs outstretched
to hanging Nikes,
Rebooks, Avias,
Converse, Adidas,

Pumas, Keds,
perhaps
a dozen more,
counter balanced
by work boots,
Justins, Dickies,
LaCross, Chippewas,
telling stories
to the wind
of the high desert,
casting slight shadows
on distant mountains,
eavesdropping
on passers-by
encased securely
in tiny metal boxes.

Ephram Pratt Reads Numbers in the Sky

Days were turning into fall
and Ephram Pratt

was counting the leaves
on the pepper plants

in his garden.
There were seventeen

on each plant,
a number meaningful

to members of
a secret society

headquartered
in Southern Sudan.

His gloved hands were red,
and he read

from a crimson scroll,
the red hair

of the Sirens of Syracuse
falling sensuously

over all the books,
from Nephi to Moroni,

scales falling from the eyes
of Salvador Dali

as he swam in the
sad rubicund ocean of salt.

When You Welcome a Stranger,
Consider Him Your Most Generous Thief

Rich Ives

I ask the sun to explain
the dust it left on my hat.

In the heated air there are so many
things to do wrong. With each one

there's a trail of increasing inertia
and the bigger crime gets left behind.

You have to listen a long time to
wake them, guilty as they are of collecting

themselves from the unexplained air.
If you have to be available,

take along a little yesterday.
Don't expect tomorrow to fill you.

I don't really need a philosophy of moonlight,
but listen to the self-taught crickets

explaining why everywhere that matters is here.
We always have a meeting later to explain

why we have a later meeting.
The real criminals eventually fall apart

and go to sleep although the sleep no longer
belongs to them. An owl in his puffy trousers

fluffs his upper body stump and circulates
his vision, a far more local and piercing yellow

than any child's impression of sunlight.
That's the way it is with absence—

you have to take it in to be
taken in by it.

Breakdown of a Truckdriver

Arthur Gottlieb

All day I deadhead West
hauling my empty refrigerator rig
like a long coffin.

At dusk the road throws curves
I can't catch. Cat's eye
reflectors leap from railings
to claw me blind.

Knuckles gripping the wheel
go white as ten ghosts' skulls.
I double clutch my gut
to get over the last hill,
hoping home will loom somewhere
in the final stretch.

When an outburst of brights
from oncoming cars hit me
head on, I pull in to this
lonely truckstop motel.

Here I have nothing
but the past to look forward to.
Millions of miles under my belt
knot my stomach into unlucky
concrete cloverleaves.

The vacancy sign still beckons
with a whore's wink as I drive
myself crazy up a wall,
cracked into a thousand plaster
maps, ribbons of road unwinding
in my rearview mirror, turning me,
like a speedometer, back to zero.

All the ground I've covered
just a mound of dirt now
in a dream of me, buried bones
with only an ambulance siren crying
on the cold shoulder of the road,
its red cross my grave's solitary marker.

Egg And I

Doug Bolling

They tell me life began as an egg.
A small mouth concealed below a rock
not far from the sea.

They tell me to travel through the sands
with their great thirst.
Through the mountains holding the sky
in their rough palms.

They tell me not to quibble with the
blackbirds circling overhead looking for
my hair.

Go gently they say. Walk on your stilts
like a giraffe searching for its mate.

Fill an artistic bottle with sea water
they say and carry it to the quiet valley
where the grasses whisper their terrible
secrets, all the secrets of their years.

Be humble they say. Recall your short
passage in the valleys, the sands, the sea
that has its eye on you as you swim naked
in the cinematic surf, in the upper waves.

Listen for the moon they say.
Its voice quiet as a sleeping lion
after repast, after the dreams of conquest
have subsided.

When you find the egg they say
lie down beside it and wait,
wait for the birth of yourself,
the birth of the final words.

Dad's Wheels

Haesong Kwon

Nada y pues nada
says the wet
leaves

of the carport pavement.
Tomorrow

the wet leaves
are gone, and I'm under

the hood of his ride
clipping wire after

wire, and because they are
bastards, his cheapo flip

flops are clapping,
but the ruddy

plunger in his hand
has lowered its head.

Ashes made of clams fly
into the streets, eventually.

Now that I'm on my own
I catch the bus to work, listen

to a load of baseball
and stare at the browning

bananas on the kitchen
counter. *Why'd*

you get them
then, snaps the wayside

leaves and I'm all, *quit*
fucking around, dad

you're no leaves
you're my

Thanks

Maybe you are seven hundred
yards away. You believe these frozen
crystals

are ideas, and liken them to the orphan
notes of your kindergarten triangle.

You carry an egg
in your propped-up hand
having kept it from breaking
all day long.

You walk to the front
of your grade school auditorium
to get your Citizen-of-the-Month certificate

carrying the egg.
What were you like when your hair
was brown and straight?

Thanks
for letting me know that wasp eggs reside still
in Nabisco fig newtons.

That the single cloud is just a long-board
and cruising on it, the long-bearded hermit
yonder, close to visible.

An Area Bounded by Three Surface Streets

John F. Buckley

Our neighborhood blossoms lutescent with dry-aged
sides of sunburn on slow-walking grandmothers and

immature dandelions. Frozen cubes of ground basil
lose their flavor in every home freezer. It has one pair

of new Wal-Mart sneakers thrown over a power line
outside the apartment complex, size nine, I'd guess.

It acts as a magnet for uncle-touching Santa Ana winds
that blow colder and colder each year. Our neighborhood

was meticulously designed by a master planner long after the
syphilis kicked in. Its streets arc like chip shots

intended as penalty kicks, high hidden slopes that test
brakes and cause accidents with native squirrels. But

it has no knowledge of meanness, only the rules of real-
world McDonalds Monopoly. It seems to speak to us

sometimes: *We need ice-cream socials and taco-eating*
contests to solder your lips in solidarity, hidden mikes

near the traffic cameras to record the tenor whalesongs
of your passings through me. It floats on a grimy tectonic

hubcap balanced on the back of an underground turtle,
spinning us gently along through history and space.

Pillow Head:
The Continuous Dream of Wooden Objects

Susan H. Maurer

Pillow Head
Up start worries
Flight of grey-brown moths
Guatemalan trouble dolls
Have six worries
Whisper to them
They will do what dolls will do
During the night

Awakening

Don Eckler

A mirror without shape appears
At noon in the blue water ocean

Images rise up from the depths
Silently calling, pulling my gaze down

My world focuses then closes
As I shed my clothes

Then I am drawn over the railing
Diving into the ocean and down

I move into this world mesmerized
Not sinking down

The sea is coming up, opening up
As it rises around me it embraces me

Intuitively I know the sea
Is my friend, she would never hurt me

Awakening

Reluctantly I return from her embrace
Realizing the line I crossed

I left that spiritual realm knowing now
I can call myself a sailor.

Jumpers

Tracy Burkholder

I've been obsessed with the jumpers for months. Every day, I sit in front of my computer and watch them leap.

Nineteen miles above solid ground, John Kittinger prepares. Wearing the best partial pressure suit 1960 has to offer, he stands on the open platform of the helium balloon that has lifted him to this point, high above the highest clouds. He presses down through his feet, knees bending, ankles held at a ready angle. An enormous emptiness stretches beneath him. Poised above the earth, waiting to leap, he prays. And then, with a flash of synapses, a click of kinetic energy, his body moves from poised to pushed. From jump to jumped.

Three men stand on the edge of a Norwegian cliff. As if stepping off a sidewalk, they move from earth to air. With exquisite grace, they flip backwards as they fall, taking one last glance at the ground they just abandoned. Wide sheets of fabric stretch between the legs and off the arms of the suits they wear, turning them into nylon birds. No one and nothing but their brave bird nerves push them from the nest.

Gene Sprague paces a small portion of the Golden Gate Bridge. The wind whips his long, black hair across his face. With a snap, he whips it back. Eventually, his pacing stops. He is unaware that a documentarian is filming him from the edge of the bay, silent witness to the suicides committed from the bridge. Gene leans out over the railing and looks into the frigid, unforgiving waves. A gray-haired couple stands nearby photographing their moment amongst the giant red cables. Gene turns his back on the bay and lifts himself onto the ledge the way a boy would hop onto a low wall. The couple doesn't seem to notice, maybe because it happens so quickly. With barely a pause, Gene straightens to standing and falls backwards into the air. More air. Water.

Fixed to freefall. Safety to surrender. That moment of transition runs in a twitchy tape loop through my brain. Their feet press into the solidness beneath them, ready to spring and then they spring. Months ago, I watched a clip posted on Facebook of men leaping from a mountain ledge. Now I seek out DVD's and YouTube videos, less interested in the falling and flying than I am in that irreversible moment. You can't stop jumping half way through a jump.

But you can, with a few clicks of a keyboard, fix the moment and turn it back. I return John Kittinger to his balloon, the wingsuit men to solid ground, and Gene Sprague to the world of the living. I don't pretend that I'm keeping them safe, or that I'm keeping myself from seeing their fate. I do it to try and identify what makes that moment possible, as if their bravery is not only a virtue I can admire but a skill I can acquire through sheer repetition of viewing. Their legs lift them from one medium to another and I watch as if it were a waltz I might someday have the grace to perform. I bring stillness to the instant when their bodies pitch over the edge while their feet remain planted, touching the ground but no longer attached to it.

That is the moment I fear. That terrible slant.

I am a coward. Always have been. The only jumps I make are over puddles, the only dives into chlorinated pools. The skateboard I bought with the encouragement of my high school boyfriend rarely left the driveway for fear of a skinned knee. Lounging on the sandy edge of my favorite river spot, I keep my back to the reckless teenagers upstream plunging from the high rocks. I was built for languor, not danger.

Recently, a friend told me that she went skydiving on a whim and can't wait to go again. "I'm an adrenalin junkie," she said.

I cringed. "I think I'm allergic to adrenalin."

And there lies the problem, the reason I keep watching these videos: My particular kind of cowardice extends beyond the common aversions to speed, heights and bodily harm. Cowards of my ilk know how it feels to tilt over a precipice, our blood rich with fear even while sunk into the cushions of a comfy chair.

This is the kind of coward I am: In the whole of my formal education, I probably asked less than five questions. Even as an elementary school girl I found that raising my hand in class made me numb with terror. Like a first-time skydiver who fails to leave the plane, I felt physically incapable of lifting my arm.

The written word became my salvation. At first, I left notes for my mother with questions I was too scared to pull from my lips: *What do I do when I get my period? I want to learn how to dance, will you let me take a class?* In high school, I wrote letters to the boys I had crushes on rather than flirt with them at McDonald's the way everyone else did. Still older, I confessed my attraction to not one, but two different men in conspicuously placed notes delivered under the cover of dark.

In a video titled *Fearless—The Jeb Corliss Story*, Mr. Corliss, a veteran skydiver and jumper, describes the moments before a jump this way: "The fear is…a hurricane inside your head. Every nerve ending is saying *don't do this*." Mr. Corliss was diagnosed with counterphobia, a psychological condition where he seeks out situations or objects that he fears. His heartbeat rattles the back of his throat, his body tells him to back away, but instead he steps closer. He leaps.

Mr. Corliss, having gone through years of depression and suicidal thoughts, described his initial feelings towards jumping this way: "Either I'll die, and I don't want to be here anyway, or I'll live and have done something amazing."

As a young adult, I followed a kind of coward's guide to suicidal urges: Sit with the unmedicated residents of Boston's public benches and listen to their rants. Wander alone through the moon-made shadows of suburban playgrounds, college arboretums and quiet urban streets. Court a more delineated form of death among the gravestones of old cemeteries.

And then there was the subway trick. I would stand with the curve of my shoes half way into the yellow line that marked the edge of the Boston T platform. There I waited for that nearly indistinguishable instant when the subway car passed from tunnel to station to me, followed by a gray rush that blew the hair from my eyes and filled my nose with gusts of dirt and piss. The screeching, rhythmic roar crossed the narrow space between the train's motion and my own stillness.

The trick was to hold that stillness. To stay put. Not lean out into the deadly smack, but imagine how any one part or the whole damn lot could be taken. Just like that.

And just like that, the train would stop, the doors would open. In the cold, white light of the car, I'd find a seat. Crowded by other commuters, all I'd feel was the closeness of that metal, the obliterating blur that lifted the fine ends of my nerves like a breeze.

Being a coward kept me alive. If I'd been braver I might have jumped. Of course, if I'd been braver, I might have introduced myself to that group of interesting-looking people who always ate in the same dining hall as me. I would have said yes to more invitations. I would have raised my hand. Cowardice kept me creeping out to the edge where I'd fill with that hurricane of fear. I'd crouch there for a while then slink back into my life.

I'm no less of a coward now than I was then. I've simply arranged my life in a way that keeps adrenalin out of the picture as much as possible. My thrill seeking is confined to the rare roller coaster ride, the occasional scary movie. Activities that may not even produce adrenalin, only some minor chemical cousin.

These days, the crutches of email, texting and social networking have tilted my fears back to the spoken word. All it takes is the thought of having to call a plumber, chat with strangers at a party or even maneuver around an awkward silence with a friend. A few drops of adrenalin are all I need to feel like there's nothing between me and a long way down.

In many ways, I've learned to listen to my body and interpret its signals. I know by the first ghostly aches around my elbow that I need to cut back my computer time or risk stirring up months of painful tendonitis. I know when I get weepy over cat food ads that I need more sleep and a break from the onslaught of dreary world news. But the signals my body sends when staring at the digits of a stranger's phone number or when approaching an acquaintance on the sidewalk make no sense. My brain scrambles and leaps, trying to find a reason why those numbers don't need to be called. Not now. Not ever. My heart hops up higher in my chest as I search my purse, tie my shoe or even duck into a nearby shop to avoid the pain of eye contact and casual hellos. And there's always the thin sweat that worries its way through the most thorough layer of antiperspirant.

It doesn't usually get to this point, of course, because my cowardice is more clever now. I know to avoid the ledge altogether, convinced not only that I don't need to jump from it, but that I don't even need to check out the view. As I write this, a list of potential business clients I need to call are typed out on a computerized sticky note. The list is nothing but a thin, turquoise bar I barely notice until I click on it and it expands into a taunting, four-inch square. It's been sitting there for months and my powers of avoidance haven't even begun to be challenged.

Others have it worse. Some people have full-blown social phobias that keep them trapped in their houses. Some have trimmed down their lives into friendless, loveless slivers of isolation in order to avoid the panicky slant of social interaction. The internet can be a balm for such people, providing connection without panic. It can also be a suffocating blanket that keeps the shy person from ever being challenged.

Recently, in my own internet wanderings, I came across a research study for the socially phobic. Participants follow a 9-week program called Social Fitness Training that was developed at the Stanford University Shyness Clinic. Immediately, I pictured the clinic's waiting room full of bowed heads and twitchy fingers. So blatantly admitting to your shyness as to walk through a door with the word right on it got my heart fluttering a bit. Thankfully, this was an internet based program. Staring at the shoes of my fellow shymates would be unnecessary.

I circled the cursor over the link, wondering if I should click it. The whole thing made me terribly uncomfortable and yet there I was of my own volition at www.shyness.com. I debated erasing all tell-tale signs of self-helpery from my internet history and going back to YouTube. Instead, I imagined Jeb Corliss standing at the edge of a cliff with every nerve shot through with DON'T. I thought of Gene Sprague, with only one courageous leap left in his legs. I laughed nervously as I told my boyfriend what I was about to do. The laughter got higher pitched as soon as I pushed "send" and the email agreeing to participate in the study was sent off to the researcher.

Later that day, I typed John Kittinger's name into an image search engine and copied my favorite picture. I then clicked over to Facebook and replaced my profile photo with what I had found: Kittinger framed by the ledge of his 19-mile high balloon, jumping back into the world.

Reservoir

Jean McDonough

Lilly pads dot the water
like floating green and yellow coins,
red-winged blackbirds dart
back and forth,
blue and orange dragonflies hover
in tandem above the clear water—
it's quiet except for the crunching
of my footsteps on the gritty path.
It's a sparkling day, bright blue sky,
cool air, warm sun and I know somehow
that I'm being asked to pay attention.
I am content to walk and look and listen
and breathe, taking it all in.
Simple beauty, nature's beauty
always has a way of soothing me
like nothing else. When I die,
I hope I am sitting outside
under a tree, a warm breeze
on my face or by the water watching
the clouds shift-shape by.

In a moment a snake will suddenly emerge
from the brush in a panic;
in a moment I won't be able to speak
as the long, thick, black shape makes
a bee-line right toward me—
I will scream one long deafening scream
as if my mouth were being torn open
by something sharp-taloned.
Then at the end of a long screeching exhale
when all breath is gone,
when the only thing left
is the incomprehensible
silence,
only then will I become aware
of mercy.

In the death of that moment, mercy
comes forth and carries me
to the next breath, mercy
carries me back to the grass,
to the path, to the snake,
which, at that moment, abruptly turns away
as if by some inexplicable order
it must obey, and vanishes.

Holy Cards

At the funeral home,
you sit in a proper chair,
in a proper room, speaking
in proper tones about the proper burial
of your mother. *Do I have this right?*
Yes, this is right. A few minutes ago,
you were discussing other things:
thechurchtheservicethetimethecemeterytheobituarythelimousine
The limousine comes in two sizes, service
for six or service for ten.

You count on your fingers
the important people.
Is that everyone? You think so.
In a day or two, you will ride sideways
in the ten-seater limousine, feeling
confused and disoriented. The once familiar
streets and buildings, the straight-ahead view,
will be blocked and you will think
the driver is going the wrong way.
Will he drive too fast? No, he will drive
too slowly.

You must pick out the funeral cards.
They are provided by the funeral home;
they are complimentary up to a certain number.
You are told that they will print
your mother's name, date of birth, death
on the back. You are allowed to pick
from a box containing samples.
Is that Italian Renaissance?

The cards are taken out of the box
for a closer look—spread out on the floor.
You remember other times as children
when you and your sister spent time like this
on the floor playing games, drawing pictures,
curling each other's hair. One Christmas morning,
you played with your sister under the tree
with the bride dolls that were all the rage.

Your mother must have stayed up late
many nights sewing
the heavy white satin with seed pearls
and lace. The dolls were slender
adult-looking figures with dreamy eyes,
rosy cheeks, long dark hair.
When we weren't playing
with the bride dolls, they were positioned
in the center of our twin beds
with their full satin skirts arranged
in a circle around them—fussy, shiny,

elaborate. A minute ago
you were sitting in a proper chair,
in a proper room, speaking
in proper tones about the proper burial
of your mother.

Below Reason

There's no way to keep it up any longer—
better to sit and watch the snow fall
watching intently
your eye catching a single flake
following its path up a little,
down, to the left, and down again
your eye not sure what it saw in the first place
yet quick to pick up another flurry
over and over
until your eyes begin to flutter
and you realize you're slipping a little
so you pull your focus back
eye the whole scene.
But soon your eye begins to trace them again
and no matter how many times
you raise your eyes up
they follow the movement back down
below the view, because they have to
because resistance:

might stop the world.

A Red Fox, Killed

Erick Aare

We like our old country road,
Though it's gravel and rough, hard on a car.
We like to walk this road with its little traffic
As it parallels the paved highway.
Those who come this way must come for a reason
Or by mistake, led astray.
But yes, we do see roadkill sometimes even here,
A barn owl half-alive in the ditch,
A deer with a broken leg. Both died.

At the zigzag
On our usual daily walk we were startled
By the body of a red fox
Lying dead on the verge, freshly killed.
Well, we don't have red foxes here.
We've seen our grey fox pass by a time or two.
We all know that a fox is too wily to be killed by traffic
On a lonely road where no one can speed.

Of course, running over a skunk is common practice.
We smell them regularly, but skunks can barely run,
Don't run, challenge you on the trail.

Consider themselves invulnerable.

(One time on a walk, I met another skunk

With a litter who abandoned them at my approach.

The kittens, all five, curled into a furry ball in the middle of the road.

I shooed them off and saved them then, but over the weeks

Would sadly see one here or one there run over

Until they were mostly gone I think.)

But a fox, a red fox, even though an alien,

Who would kill a fox?

We stopped to examine the body,

Those beautiful ears, that magnificent tail, those legs too slender.

We ask each other,

How did this creature come to be here.

How did this lovely beast come to die here.

We have lost something here, I think,

Though in the treetop a hundred blackbirds sing.

The Closing of Joe's Bar

Kait Heacock

"Hello, yes, hi. I'd like to report a missing person." It was funny how you had to call the non-emergency line for something like this, funny trying to tell the parents and wife of a missing person that this was a non-emergency.

"And now you say nobody has heard from your son in two days?" The policewoman's voice over the phone was calm, soothing, like he imagined a phone sex operator's voice would sound, not that Gary had ever called a phone sex line before.

He nodded and then realized she couldn't see his movement and said quickly, "Yes, ma'am."

"Has he ever or does your son now drink and/or use drugs? Excuse me for my forwardness, but I have to ask."

"That's quite alright. Part of the job, I know. Yes, to both, alcohol mostly, but his past, well it hasn't been perfect."

"Does he have a history of this, these disappearing acts, let's call them?"

"When he was younger, in college, he'd disappear on binges every now and again and it would be a little while until we heard from him."

"Mmmhmm," she said like she expected it. "It sounds to me like he might be on another binge. You'd be surprised how often that's the case." Now she sounded like one of those types who don't trust men, one of those lesbian types. "You'd be surprised." You'd be surprised that he had been faithful to his wife for over twenty-five years, but that didn't mean it weren't true.

"With all due respect, officer, it's different this time." He liked calling her "officer"; it felt funny saying it to a lady.

"How so?"

"Well see, his wife, my daughter-in-law, she's in the hospital right now. She's about to deliver his baby. He left two nights ago to get a bite to eat, and he hasn't come back since."

"Now why would your son skip out on his wife when she's in the hospital about to have his kid?"

"You got me, ma'am."

"Listen sir, I'm going to get your report in right now and send someone out to your house for further questioning. If you can give me your location we can probably get someone out in the next forty-five minutes."

He hung up the phone wishing his part were over. Kim jumped up from the kitchen table and he knew she would make a run for the vacuum cleaner—even in times of trouble you have to clean the house for company. Mostly he felt embarrassed about the whole mess. Even if he could never give Kim the best life, even if their house was in Shoreline and not Seattle, and maybe a little too close to Highway 99, even so, it was their house, bought and paid for, and now a cop was about to show up at his door in front of all his neighbors because his son up and disappeared right before his wife went into labor. Gary didn't think it was as bad as Kim and little Megan thought it was, so bad they made him call the police to file the report. Kim couldn't bear to make the phone call and you couldn't expect Megan to do it, especially not since this morning when her water broke.

Kim paused with the vacuum. "After the police leave, we have to get to the hospital. I know Megan's parents don't want to see us right now, not since it's *our* son that did this to her, but we have to show our support, to everyone, especially this baby."

The way she said "our son," it was more like she said, "Your son," like this whole thing was his fault just because he was a man too. But they both raised Chris. They may not have been able to give him the world on a bus driver's salary, but they damn sure didn't raise him to disappear on his wife a year into their marriage, especially not *now*, with the baby just about to join the world, in a fatherless hospital room.

He thought the week had started off bad enough, what with the flyers showing up in the neighborhood. "Save Joe's Bar" and "Don't Let Go of a Neighborhood Treasure." Joe's Bar, the same little shit hole he had been coming to after work for fifteen years now, had it been that long? You don't go to college, your dad's a retired bus driver, and you find out your girlfriend has one on the way, what else could Gary have done but settle down, settle into the working man's life? All he ever wanted was a cold beer after work. He had never asked for much after school. Football had been good to him but not great. All he wanted to do was take care of Kim and the baby, that's why the wedding happened so fast, in the little Baptist church on the hill, because there was only so much time before she would start to show. He worked himself to the bone day in and day out with his "Hello" and "Goodbye" and "Do you need a transfer?" Best he could have hoped for Chris was that he would be smart enough to get through college, wouldn't end up driving the line through the University District and have to see too many spoiled kids showing him what life could have been like if he were smarter, or luckier.

"What will it be today, Mr. Harrison?" The bartender asked when he sat on his stool. His stool—tall mahogany, to match the bar, but a little wobbly in one leg; they never did get that fixed.

"The usual, Becky. You know some things never change."

He never saw Becky on his line, although she told him once that she was studying for her Master's over at UW. She wanted to be a writer. That was cute, he thought, and the way she cut her hair short like Peter Pan and covered her arms with tattoos. Becky was a lesbian, she had told him more than once, one of those very cool kinds that smoked more than he did—very popular amongst this generation below him. He wondered if she were a true lesbian or if she'd ever been with a man. Maybe she was just one of those experimental girls who rebelled too young against her parents. Maybe she'd drop this whole tough act if she just had a good screw.

"Some things do, I know you know that from the look on your face," she said and placed the cold glass on the counter, not spilling one bit of foam as she pushed it towards him. He didn't understand her but she poured a beer better than most.

"You mean this," he said and slapped a flyer on the counter, torn off a telephone pole, little bits of tape on the corners, evidence. "Do you want to explain?"

"Don't give me that tone. You know as well as anyone I can't afford to be out of a job. This job may not be glamorous, but it sure as hell pays the bills."

"Well, who should I ask? Joe?" For the last year and a half that Becky had been his bartender, after fat Tony died of a heart attack and Louis moved to the east coast nearly a decade ago, she always knew when Gary had had one too many because he always asked who Joe really was. It didn't happen often because he was one of those stiff, fatherly types, but when it did she told him Joe had been a cowboy or a bullfighter or a boxer long before Joe's Bar. He didn't think anyone knew Joe or there was even a Joe to know, but he figured that if someone did it had to be the bartender. It must have been a secret they told them in training.

"There's nobody to ask, Mr. Harrison. The lease ends in a week and patrons can rally all they want, but this neighborhood is changing. The landlord wants us out. This place is a little too blue collar for the condos down the street. They want something more upscale."

After three more beers, beers of solace, Gary told Becky, "I want Joe to fix this."

"You know Joe can't do that, Mr. Harrison, he died in the space shuttle back in '86, just after launch. He should have stuck with bartending, I guess."

That was just five days ago, a regular Monday. Now it was a Friday and he was about to be a grandpa and his only son was gone. Joe's Bar was only a fifteen-minute drive, but Kim wouldn't let him go, not with the police on their way. He cracked a can and let the bubbles settle his stomach. The vacuum whooshed around the house right up until the doorbell rang. Kim hid upstairs the whole twenty minutes the officer sat in the living room with Gary. He forgot to throw out the beer before opening the door, but didn't want to ditch it with the officer inside—the way they made him feel guilty when he didn't even do anything. Instead, he held it self-consciously on his knee as he described Chris's height, eye color, and visible tattoos or scars. He forgot about the little one above his eyebrow, the one he gave Chris when he was sixteen and got caught stealing liquor from a convenience store. That was the last time they had fought like that, in the kitchen, with fists, and Kim had said, "I refuse to stand between you two anymore.

Just go ahead and kill each other." And they did stop, both out of equal dependence on the woman, and for all her talk about women's liberation and going out and getting that part-time job at the library (not like a real librarian, you have to go to school for that), she needed them too, her boys.

When Gary and Kim arrived at the maternity ward an hour later, they found out there was another little boy in their world, a son, a grandson. Even though little Megan's uptight mother stared at Gary like he must have been a devil, he didn't let her spoil it for him, holding this little boy like he had held Chris twenty-five years ago. And he thought that if Chris could just hold this baby he would know what it felt like to be a father, to want to stop living your life because you have to live for this kid now. Gary had been a really great bartender when he found out Kim was pregnant, the really good kind that listened to customers like a therapist, but he quit it for Chris, found that day job, a different place to listen to people and all their problems.

He and Kim were shunned from the hospital because of visiting hours. She didn't want to go home and made plans to have dinner with her sister. "Why don't you go to Joe's tonight, Gary? You need to get out of the house too and it's closing soon, isn't it?"

When he arrived at the bar it was still early enough to beat the Friday night crowd, the younger kids with fresh IDs who thought bars like this were ironic. Mostly, it was just Becky and him. She had to put up with him because he was a regular.

"You've got three days before this place closes, Mr. Harrison, feel like trying something new?"

"No, Becky. I've had enough excitement today, just give me a Budweiser."

"What kind of excitement does a man like you have?"

He told her about Chris, one to make her feel guilty, and two because every customer needed a therapist.

"I'm really sorry to hear that. How's the baby doing?"

"He's great, you know, as far as babies go. Healthy and happy, it seems. Not a care in the world."

"You've got to try your best to think of that."

"You mean instead of that little shit son of mine?"

"Be careful what you say. At least wait until you know he's alright before you hate him." Now he felt guilty, that twinge in the chest that maybe his son died before him. What's a parent to do without a son?

At home he found Kim crying on the phone with Megan. Still no word from Chris and Megan was cleared to leave the hospital in the morning. All these people lined up in his world—women mostly, with their tears and the way they look at you like maybe you've made one too many wrong choices in life—all these people, and he didn't know how to fix a single one of them. He threw a chair at the wall that wouldn't get picked up for days. There was nothing else to do but wait.

On Saturday Gary and Kim were allowed over to Chris and Megan's apartment (maybe they should just have called it Megan's place). Her parents were out grocery shopping while the guilty parents stopped by. They had to take the blame. Without Chris around, there was nobody else. The baby slept, nameless, while Gary and Kim watched Megan teeter around the small apartment unpacking and tidying things up—women always had to clean something in a crisis.

"We just want to say that we're really sorry, Megan," Gary said, like they had practiced in the car ride over. "We just didn't see a thing like this coming."

"I suppose you never do. It's always a little different looking from the outside."

He wanted so badly to ask. Was there something that made Chris leave? Maybe Megan told Kim on the phone, but neither looked like they planned to tell him. He'd never understand women and their secrets. After the apartment and seeing that baby asleep in the bassinet, oblivious, Gary felt compelled to have a drink.

"Any word from the kid?" Becky asked beer glass in hand.

"Not a syllable."

Gary had never seen the Saturday crowd before. He was a workweek drinker. They were mostly younger, still looked fresh out of college, frightened and prematurely haggard. He didn't remember looking that way at twenty-five. His generation, they took life as it came to them, didn't expect much more than what they could work for. These kids today, they expected the world to be handed to them on a silver platter.

Gary drank too much that night, didn't want to face Kim at home, not with her so sad that maybe she had failed as a mother, not wanting to show his stupid drunken face like he had so many times before. How many times had Kim helped him into bed, tucked him under covers like her own son? Did she ever tell him to say his prayers? No, he must have overheard her saying that to Chris. These mothers, so protective of their boys.

"Maybe it's time you called it a night, Mr. Harrison," Becky suggested in that phone sex operator voice she too put on when she needed to calm a man, calm him at least. Did he look that drunk?

"Maybe you should call it a night, Becky. Why don't you let me take you home tonight? Joe's Bar is closing, what you got to lose?"

"My self-respect, Mr. Harrison. And you could lose your wife for saying something like that. Go home. She needs you now."

"But what about what I need? Nobody ever thought of that. My son ditches and leaves all these women for me to deal with on my own. Maybe I should run too. All I ever wanted was a place of my own. Now that the bar's closing, it doesn't feel like there's much reason to stay."

She breathed out heavily, like a big sigh of frustration. "It's just a bar."

"When you get to be my age, Becky, it's everything."

She shouted last call to the bar. When he turned around, most of them had already cleared out. Go back to your mothers, children, they'll protect you.

Gary turned back to the bar. "Tell me Becky, who was Joe? And you better make it pretty damn good this time or else no tip." He only meant it to be funny, their last laugh. He didn't want to be one of those old men who cry at bars.

She set the glass she was cleaning down on the bar. "You know Gary, here's a little secret for you. It wasn't ever Joe at all. It was Jo without the "e," and she was the meanest dike you ever saw. I'm talking part truck driver part WNBA. She added the "e" when she opened the bar so that long after her death she could really stick it to schmucks like you. Because she knew that even after forty-six years of business, there would still be men like you who depended on this place, who looked to it like a sanctuary, where they could be men and they could treat women like shit, and it would probably be men like you who saw this place to the ground, but every time you drank to that last drop of beer, you'd be drinking beer because of a lesbian."

"That's not true Becky, you know it." He wished he could have had a daughter.

A cute blond in a too-tight dress sat down at the empty bar stool two away from Gary. Maybe his luck was bound to change after all. She looked in his direction and smiled.

"Excuse me," Becky said and threw the towel onto the bar, real dramatic like, like Gary had seen in those soapy ten o'clock dramas Kim liked to watch so much. Who needs to watch it on television when you've got enough of it to deal with at home?

Gary watched Becky move over to the new girl, ready to take her order. But then she leaned over the counter and laid one on her, open mouthed kissed the girl right in front of him. His glass of beer slipped out of his hand and if it weren't for him just barely holding it above the bar, it would have shattered right there in front of everyone. He had enough trouble getting by with this crowd around him getting younger and younger. He didn't need to start dropping things on top of it.

Fifteen years coming to this place and this was how it would end: His jerk of a son doing God knows what out there, while that pretty young wife of his, all waif-like and tired and in need of care after childbirth waited for him at home, and she probably wouldn't even hold it against him, his little spree, Kim at home falling asleep sitting up in bed, a beauty magazine strewn across her chest like she thought an article on the top ten butt firming exercises would reverse time, and him, sitting alone at the bar while the prettiest thing he ever saw in a dress kissed another girl, his girl even, his Becky.

He put a bigger tip on the counter than usual, at the end of a long run, when it counted, and asked Becky where she planned on going now.

She walked slowly, running a towel along the top of the bar, as she moved towards him. "Well, I'm not done yet, still have another year before my M.F.A. But I have a job lined up at a bar over on Capitol Hill."

"Over there, huh? Like one of those gay bars?"

"Yes, Mr. Harrison, one of those."

"Well, I'll tell you, I'd sooner stay at home and save my money than spend it at a place like that."

"I trust you would."

He collected his keys and stood up. "Thanks for everything Becky. See you in church some day."

"Yeah, some day, Mr. Harrison. Take care."

Their goodbye that night felt like a real goodbye, and even though he didn't go to the bar on Sundays (the Lord's day, after all), he thought maybe he could swing by for one last drink after work on Monday, closing day. He wanted to avoid any of the noise and sentimentality of Joe's closing, but at five o'clock and nearing a week of Chris's disappearance, Gary couldn't find a reason to go home, not yet.

But then his cell phone rang on the drive from work and it was Kim and she said, "Chris called Megan. He's done. He needs a ride. Megan can't do it, not with the baby, and Lord knows I can't do it." He knew that if he were to ever resent Chris for anything, it would be that he called home on Monday and not Tuesday.

When he picked him up, Chris smelled like body odor and cologne, awful like he hadn't showered in a week, and he wore the same clothes he left Wednesday night in.

"What in God's name were you thinking?"

"I wasn't really, that much. I just needed to get out. It was all closing in on me, Megan and the baby coming, and I got scared. I didn't do much, I swear, just called up a few old friends from school and went to a few parties."

"Went to a few parties? For five goddamn days? She had the baby Chris, do you even care."

"Yes dad, I do care. That's why I need to get home. My son needs a name. She wouldn't do it without me."

"For the life of me, Chris, I'll never understand how you could do this." He kept his hands gripped on the steering wheel, his eyes on the road. You can't look at a person the same after they've let you down.

Chris pulled at his seat belt. "You must know what I felt. You've been through the same thing, not knowing what's coming, feeling like you have no say in your own life. I know you had to have been scared too."

"But the difference," he wanted to say, "Was that I didn't run." He didn't say it, though. Maybe he did run, in a way.

When he parked the car in front of the apartment building, he got out and stood in front of Chris. Chris stepped onto the curb—never quite as tall as his dad. Gary didn't know whether to shake his hand or hug him, thankful he was home but mad as hell for leaving in the first place. Chris moved first, put his arms around Gary's shoulders. What could he do but hug him back? He had to hug him, his only son.

The bar closed down, even with all the thoughtful flyers posted around the neighborhood and the local news coverage. It became another memory, like Gary suspected he would someday. They opened up a restaurant in the space, some real fancy place with regional cheese plates and twenty-five dollar pieces of salmon, the type of place Kim dropped hints towards around their anniversary. Even if the restaurant couldn't hold a candle to a good steakhouse or even if it someday turned into another coffee house with art on its walls that would never sell, the bar would still be gone. Forgotten.

It was gone, but what could he do? The world still had to spin.

The War Reporter Paul Watson's South African Psychiatrist Tells a Story

Dan O'Brien

I'm sitting in an Eames chair. I'm scribbling
on a legal pad. But when I was fresh
out of medical school they sent us away
to the border. With headlines proclaiming,
We are not in Angola! Hours later
you're flying, red incandescent floating
flares like angels in the trees. Descending
till white soldiers appear. Left with nothing
but my knife and a handgun. Sunbathing
on our stretchers, listening to our Walkmen,
when we hear a mine explode a cougar
will be dinner. Daubing bug bites by day,
riding by night through the thorn brush hunting
the Black Threat. When you are dead your family
will only be informed you've disappeared
along a border that doesn't exist.

Tranquil

Michael Torok

I don't care
that I've spent the last twenty-two
years trying to reclaim
the inability to say no. Trying
to get you to kiss me again
in the front seat of the car;
I don't even know whose
car it was.
You've asked.

It is the hollow I've found
after unchanged voices slip through
from an unwanted past.

It is the noise between the music
played too loud as I drink myself
to sleep that surrounds me.

It is the ghost of you lying
curled into me, my arms hugging
the morning's pillow.

It is the empty of the desert
that same morning promising a clear
ride into New Mexico mountains.

It is the thrum of the woman
who never leaves me between my legs
pulling me into headlight drunk altitude.

It is finding hope on the roadside
in a pile of rabbit, vomit, and anxiety
before seeing you again.

It is the tranquil of the overwrought.
And I thank you, under bruised sky,
for giving it back.

Laundry

There is something
strange about folding my son's clothes
when he is not here.
It is quiet mourning,
a remembrance, that allows
renewal.

I am forced to think
of all the times I've not
lived up to his smile. Allowed
his tears to fall before comforting
hurt feelings. Folding his pirate
blanket,

realizing he'll outgrow
it soon. I have one chance. Frightening
myself into immobility as I consider
his absence. A month in which I must
correct so much of my own
behavior.

He parts from me, taken
on father's day almost every year,
to spend solid time with his mother,
to waltz around a city full of whispers,
full of temptations, he *runs cars*, a game
he has made up.

He races barefoot
down the sidewalk as cars turn
onto Woodrow. I am left to worry
on broken glass and rusted nails,
on slippery perches atop washed SUV's,
on wet cheeks I cannot comfort.

It is this time, when I am still,
when I miss the broken silence he fills
with a voice of questions
and authoritative guesses. When
the silence is here,
so is the darkness.

Mr. Velvet Ears

Susan Duke

Late morning sun peeked through maple leaves dancing in the summer wind. The hound lifted his massive head to read scents on the breeze. Rabbits that had scurried in the night were long gone to hide in burrows in the day. A solitary raccoon must have visited the neighboring cornfield and poked along the backyard fence during a midnight scavenger raid.

Petey's keen nose and brain received, sorted and stored all this aromatic data like a computer. He might shuffle out after dark tonight to investigate, his foot-long velvety ears acting like fans, blowing odors up from the ground to his nose. His wide nostrils flared as he lay in the soft grass and considered it.

Maybe not. Basset hounds are creatures of habit. After a supper of canned Alpo, he would probably lounge on the treated pine deck until the woman or his girl let him into the house.

Never the man, though. He would most likely ignore Petey or complain about that darn dog being underfoot. Useless, darn dog's good for nothing.

Petey's even temperament didn't include regret, but his intelligence made him aware of who favored him. The woman fed him morning and night and talked to him every day. She was always there when he needed companionship. He often did.

His girl was the special one, and he loved her unconditionally. From as far back as he could remember they had forged an unbreakable bond. She would sneak the mournful-looking pup into her bed where he would snuggle and inhale her scent. When the noisy, yellow school bus opened squeaky doors, he would be at the end of the driveway waiting for her each afternoon. They would run and play until both flopped on the lawn.

His girl could do no wrong, although at times she seemed too busy for him. He would thump his white-tipped tail on the floor to get her attention as she sat at the kitchen table, scratching on paper. Her left arm would reach down to rub his chest. He craved her hands on him as much as he wanted food. She would stroke his long ears until he knew life couldn't get any better. It had been this way for years.

The only place Petey refused to follow her was into the pool. She would splash him and laugh as he wrinkled his nose. The chemicals caused him to sneeze. He stood low set at fourteen and a half inches with a wide chest and heavy bones. His powerful legs could dog paddle, but as with many of his breed, Petey balked at getting wet.

Now, without opening his eyes, he knew his girl was in the pool. He could hear her happy sounds as she cooed to the little one. The baby produced its own scent that Petey memorized because his girl seemed to adore the strange little creature.

That was another thing that had angered the man. "Now we have to raise her darn kid. As if I don't work hard enough to put food on the table, I gotta feed a baby that should have never been born."

"Sssssh! Quiet, Mel, or she'll hear you."

The yelling had gone on until Petey had slunk into the backyard to escape the racket. He didn't understand why, but the tension in the house grew so much he could sense it. Sometimes when his girl cried, Petey put his brown and white head on her knee while she poured out her heart to him.

Peace ruled this morning. The man had driven off in the red truck that was off limits to everyone. The hound dozed lightly and could smell the squirrel before he heard it. The dog and the small tree-dwelling rodent played this game all summer and fall. The noisy squirrel scolded from the branches overhead as Petey snorted his disdain. He rolled on his back in a patch of prickly grass to scratch every itch.

Petey could not know since the sixth century Basset Hounds and small game were natural enemies. The abbots of St. Hubert in France had bred these peculiar-looking hounds to track and flush out quarry for hunters. This squirrel was safe.

Petey shook three feet from head to toe and stretched his hind legs. He relieved himself at the base of the tree to mark his territory and ambled across the yard to the pool area. The hot cement did not penetrate thick pads on his wide feet.

"Hi, Petey! You wanna swim with Little Mel and me?"

Petey's tail wagged as he regarded his beloved girl and her baby. No thanks. He snuffled loudly and located the only shade spot. As he hunkered down to crawl under the picnic table, his girl clutched the toddler and began to climb up the slippery wet steps. The dog kept one sleepy eye open. The little one had been known to step on ears or tail.

He jerked his head up as his girl slipped and fell backwards with a splash. He heard the thump as her head cracked on the side of the pool. He sensed this was bad, very bad.

Petey scrambled to the edge of the pool and danced back and forth. His anxious whines did not rouse his girl as she floated face down in the clear, blue water. The little one eased from her grasp and sank two feet to the bottom.

The hound rarely barked, but lessons from his ancestors routed through his brain. As if he were tracking a fox, Petey gave tongue. His deep, melodious voice split the summer morning until the woman ran from the house.

"Petey! What in heaven's name…oh my god!"

Petey did not quiet until she sat and slid into the pool. She turned the girl over and wrestled her from the water. The woman was doing something over the still body of the girl and had not thought of the little one. Petey whined and looked at the empty playpen. He could not will the crying woman to notice him. She jumped up and ran into the house. He could hear her yelling into the telephone.

With a grunt, Petey lunged into the pool. He paddled over and let himself sink, using his wide front paws as flippers. He grabbed the little one's T-shirt in his mouth and struggled to the surface. The toddler was so heavy Petey could not get up the tiled steps. Water filled his nose, and he almost went under, but he would not let go. His ears floated over his eyes so he could barely see, but he kept on paddling.

The woman rushed out of the house and screamed when she saw Petey and his sodden cargo. She leaped in to rescue the toddler with one hand and push the exhausted hound up the steps with the other. Petey regurgitated water and fell in a heap. He lay gasping on his side as strange people hurried into the backyard. He closed his burning eyes and drifted. He dreamed of a loud siren and people shouting.

He never knew what changed the man. He didn't care. All Petey realized was more love in the house. He heard no more yelling and crying, only happy sounds from the man, woman, and his girl. The man even looked at Petey now and scratched the dog's head. Sometimes he would chuckle as the little one pulled the dog's ears.

Yesterday, Petey's heart almost burst with joy. The man let the hound out the front door. Petey bunched his eyebrows as the man opened the door of the red truck and patted the seat.

"Well, come on, pup. Let's go for a ride."

As the wind sailed his ears, Petey watched the landscape whiz by. His drool blew back out of the open window as the man said, "Good dog."

Saints

Danielle Hanson

The benefit of being stone is that time
Slows. Take the saints on church tops,
Eternal contemplation of a jump. They
Look down on the tourists, on me, the occupants
Of Dante's First Level. The saints feel superior
For their height and their depth—
The Seventh Circle is for them, the eternal
Wood of suicides. The saints think for centuries,
First of the step, then of the fall,
Then of the scattering of stone.
They wonder if angels fell
With the speed of gravity or if they
Fell like seeds. They wonder if angels
Would scatter, if angels have atoms,
If angels are liquid, if angels feel at home
Above the Ninth Level. They wonder if they can aim,
Could land on me, could watch me scatter and seep
Through to Styx to be washed up among the pagans.
They wonder if the street will stop their fall.
They hope the momentum will carry them far,
Scatter them wide, stir enough dust into the wind

So they'll never fully land, so I'll breath them,
Cough, die sooner. They look down,
Feeling superior and contemplating the fall.

Self-Portrait of Brad

I was born in a room without mirrors.
I have never been to Madrid,
But on the second corner after the doors of
The Museum of the Dead, there is a wall
Where we leaned and watched the people
Before climbing the stairs. Since then
I have lost your face. The fates will return it to me.
I will make it a veil of cotton.

The Snail

It came in the form of a snail,
Dragging itself across her window as she died.
But that's not right.
She died in winter, or early spring
And it was frost dragging its body across the pane.
Her voice was the first to free itself, like a worm.
It burrowed into the walls, who woke up screaming.

Playground

Robert Levy

Dead rat clamped in its jaws, the fat squirrel
      scrabbles past see-saws, clambers up an oak,
            and deposits its prize in a hollow bole,

almost insouciantly, as though storing
      an acorn. It chitters out victory
            from its high aerie, as though declaiming

in squirrel: *We all eat our own.* Below,
      oblivious, toddlers gambol on swing sets
            and sliding ponds under the watchful gaze

of nannies who manage feeding time with
      Zip-Loc bags aswim with cheddar goldfish.
            The squirrel busily revisits its cache

in a box hedge abutting the playground:
      Amid the horrified, unwilling stares
            of mothers who collectively refuse

to believe that this, too, is nature,
    it retrieves a second rat, stockpiling
        it with casual, businesslike mien.

Gradually the playground grows silent.
    The gazes of children, nannies, parents
        follow the squirrel as it diligently

pries another dead rat from a drain pipe
    near the sandbox. Newly nervous, mothers
        bustle, collect their charges near their skirts,

as though worried that, empowered, squirrels
    might start making off with their progeny,
        potential carrion to help stave off

even the severest winter. Clutching
    strollers like battering rams, the parents
        retreat from the playground-turned-killing-field,

avert their children's faces from the carnage.
    Mommy, how come mouses is eating
        other mouses? Might as well ask why

the park is empty now, save for a lone
squirrel,
    its taut body a rude exclamation point
        silhouetted against the monkey bars.

Debt

Debt is propped between us tonight in bed
paging through our credit card statements,
tsking at our wild expenditures
on schoolbooks, groceries, galoshes
for the kids. My wife, half-perusing *Vogue*,
grows vague with inattention, gazing off
into the cobwebbed corners of the room
at Venetian jaunts and sprees to Cabo
we cannot afford. Debt gradually
woos her from her better self: In his scuffed
black bomber jacket he's that bad boy
women love to hate—switchblade lean,

a deck of Luckies rolled in his sleeve,
sporting negativity like mirror shades.
In bed he's a consummate acrobat,
manipulating her positions of defeat
to moments of ecstatic gloom.
It's no pedestrian *ménage a trois*;
I'm a mere voyeur to her bleak moods,
her diatribes on the *life-we-don't-have*,

things-we-don't-own and *ambitions-
to-which-we-cannot-possibly-aspire.*
I should, by all accounts, be livid—play
the jealous husband to the hilt, insist

he haul his Harley from our driveway
and vamoose. *Who's the man in black boots,
Daddy?* the kids inquire. I explain
that he's just Mommy's special friend
who moved in one day unannounced
to peruse the ledger of our losses.
Unmanned, I watch him ravish her
with inklings of the good life—front-row seats,
upscale bistros, diamond tennis bracelets
and fancy lingerie. How can I hope
to dislodge this interloper from our lives?
(Bribe him with the money I do not have?)

Of course, it isn't really riches
to which he aspires, but our company,
which he battens on, as lice co-exist
with their hosts, plying them relentlessly
as both a food source and a home.
Debt is now my wife's true spouse, a husband
to her steadfast gloom. We're getting on
now that I refrain from insisting
life isn't so bad (reminding her we have

our health, our children and our jobs).
I've moved to the foyer, make my bed
upon the couch. Sometimes at night

I hear their heated couplings through the walls,
her distraught, abandoned moans of grief,
and think, *What if I were suddenly rich?*
Would he finally pack his bags and go?
Or is my wife's passion for him so firm,
his vise-like hold on her so absolute,
that he'd remain despite my new-found wealth,
help her prosper in her faithlessness?

Meanwhile, Debt has made himself at home,
the fridge a mess, clothes strewn everywhere,
wet towels moldering on the bathroom floor,
his hand outstretched, demanding next month's rent.

In and Around the Mailbox

Jeff Bernstein

Wildlife have visited regularly
this late spring. Fox parents
play on the hillside,
followed by tiny cubs,
digging dirt for rodents.
A bold, fat woodchuck

climbs to the back deck
like a second story man,
ransacks china flowerpots
before the trapper
entices him into a crate
with jam and fruit.

Now he lives in Norwich,
half an hour away,
repatriated across two interstates.
Neighbors report a mother
bear and her cubs
traversed our driveway

and headed up the meadow.
I swim alone in the upper pond
two days before summer,
an August tourist in Paris. Oh,
one of the dogs joins me
for awhile, makes lazy

serpentine circles
as she trolls for sticks, but
it isn't the same as the spray
and splashes of children
when they searched
for weapons of mass destruction

that Saddam might have hidden,
found only water guns
while their laughter echoed
across to Hurricane Hill,
rural acres brimful. Once around
that corner you realize

there won't be time to read
all the books you want, things
feel different somehow. Some
mornings you forget that tune,
but it usually approaches
on the backs of afternoon

shadows as daylilies close
up shop, fewer and fewer
lightning bugs flash
in the evening meadow,
but for some reason
butterflies are everywhere.

Fiddling in the Boneyard

Rebecca Macijeski

I have everything to play.

I'll spend all day with the mountain graves
fiddling away to a packed house
here where the dead gather to listen.

Their death certificates
are diplomas of listening
marking the day their ears opened.

They continue to open, flowering above ground
as my bow draws along these old strings.
Melody springs,
greener even than their applause:
the old maples rustling their leaves.

Fireflies

Dennis Vannatta

I'd just gotten out of the car and was walking across the farmyard toward John Epps's front door when I heard a *bang*, like someone hitting a garbage can with a sledge hammer, and at the same time a moan of pain or rage or despair, or all of them at once. An animal. Except for four years at the state college in Conway and two years in the army, I've lived all my life in Prospect, Arkansas, population 1,006. You can't walk a hundred feet in any direction from Prospect without stepping on somebody's farm, but that doesn't make me a farmer. Animals? If an animal is bigger than a kitty cat, I don't want any part of it, and I would have beat a fast retreat back to the car and let John Epps come see me in my office if he had business with me, but then I thought *she* might be watching, so I steeled myself and went on up to the front door.

I hadn't gotten all the way through knocking when the door opened and there she was, Trish, my Trish. No, not mine. John's. Trish Epps.

I started to hold out my hand but stopped because I'd read in Miss Manners that the man waits for the lady to extend her hand to indicate she wants to shake. Besides, if I extended my hand and Trish wouldn't take it, then what would I do with my hand hanging in the air?

"Hi, Trish."

"He's around there," she said with a kind of circular motion of her head meant to indicate, I guess, around behind the house. No "Hi, Rick" or "Ricky." She'd called me that once. Trish Springer had called me Ricky once.

"OK," I said, like Lee said OK to Grant at Appomattox.

She couldn't have hurt me any worse if she'd cut my hand off. Not even to call me Ricky when all I'd done is love her this half century, love her every day through wars and presidential assassinations and a wife of my own and kids and grandkids, and I loved them all in my own way, tried my best even if I failed them, but Trish, Trish, not to even call me Ricky. It hurt so.

"OK," I said and raised my hand as if doffing my hat to her, only I wasn't wearing one.

I walked around the house and, *bang!* came that hammer-on-tin sound again—from a little trailer parked off to the side of the farm lot. I veered off in the other direction. Then here comes John Epps out of a Butler building, big sliding doors on front, probably his tractor shed.

I figured Miss Manners would be OK with me sticking my hand out, so I did, but John didn't take it, so I figured the Lord had set aside this day as one I wasn't going to get my hand shook on. I'd about sworn off shaking anyway after getting two different kinds of the flu last winter, but it seemed a hard thing that John Epps wouldn't shake my hand because when we were pups and ranked our friends one two three he'd always been one or two for me and I'm pretty sure I was the same for him. But that was a long time ago, 1968, our senior year at dear old Prospect High. Go Wildcats. But then things went wrong between us, I'm not exactly sure what, I'm truly not.

It went wrong between him and just about everybody, seems like. I went off to college and never heard a thing more about him except that he and Trish Springer got married about a year later, but I never saw either one of them around town when I came home summer or on breaks, and nobody else I talked to did, either. After college I got lucky number seven in the draft lottery and spent two years in Uncle Sam's legions, then came back and took over for old Auburn Larkin as the Heartland Insurance agent for the Prospect area. I still never heard anything about John or Trish and just kind of assumed they'd moved. But then one day here comes a check from John renewing his farm insurance policy, which I hadn't even realized he had.

Not long after that I ran into Terry Pfeiffer, also a farmer, and he said, sure, he saw John every once in awhile at the grain elevator or the farmers' co-op. He'd given up trying to talk to him, though.

"He's a stand-offish bastard. Won't hardly look you in the eye. He's a sharp one when it comes to the dollar, though, I'll grant him that. He's hell for the dollar."

"That just doesn't sound like John."

"No, it don't. He was as nice a guy as you'd ever want to meet in high school."

"How about Trish? You ever see her?"

"Trish?"

"His wife."

"Oh yeah, that's right. He did marry Trish Springer, didn't he? No, I haven't seen Trish Springer in years."

That would have been probably 1974. Where do the years go? They go on wings, I'll tell you that.

I'm not saying I've never seen him or Trish. You can't live in a little community like this without running into people, even if they are trying to be some kind of hermit. Since high school, I've seen my former best friend somewhere around a dozen times. I've seen Trish seven times. I can give you the dates, the places, the time of day. The weather. What she wore. Where she looked when she looked anywhere except at me.

I followed John across the farm lot. He was limping bad. I figured it was just a touch of arthritis since we both were at that age, but then I decided he didn't have the arthritis look on his face, like it's been hurting you so long you've almost forgotten about it. Whatever was hurting John was fresh enough he was still resenting it like hell.

"What happened to you?"

"What do you mean?"

I nodded at his leg. "You're limping."

"Oh. That bitch got a horn into me."

I thought he was talking about Trish and made a fist although taking a swing at him would have been way down on the list of good ideas. He was always bigger than me, plus he'd spent a lifetime working on a farm while I'd mostly sat behind a desk. If I'd taken a swing at John Epps to defend the good name of my fair lady, I would've ended up looking at that farm lot from a whole different angle.

Fortunately, before I could do something silly, it occurred to me that Trish didn't have a horn. At that moment John stopped and faced the trailer we'd just come along side of—what I'd call a horse trailer although I don't know if that's the name of it—and pointed like a prosecuting attorney and said, "She's in there." She must have heard us talking about her and didn't like it. *Bang.* I took a step back

"What is she?"

"A goddamn non-polled Hereford bitch. I was trying to load her into the chute and she got ornery and got a horn into me. Got me in the groin. Lucky she didn't take my pecker off."

"Must have hurt."

"You think?"

"Did you see a doctor?"

"Damn right. He cleaned it out and stitched me up and gave me a bunch of antibiotics so's it wouldn't get infected. Wanted to put me in the hospital, but a farmer can't go into the hospital any time you get a few stitches sewn into you."

"Still. You gotta be careful with something like that. I had hernia surgery a few years back and the doctor told me I couldn't lift more than ten pounds until it healed, so for a solid month I couldn't take a leak without somebody holding my John Thomas for me."

An old joke. John must have heard it too many times because he didn't laugh.

"So what are you going to do with her?" I said, and he said, "Sell her ass."

"At Grau's? The auction's not until tomorrow, is it? You going to leave her in there until then?"

"Why not? She's already been in there three days. Bitch should be used to it by now."

I started to say something but didn't. I didn't want to sound like some animal rights hothead. That doesn't go over well among farmers. And maybe it doesn't hurt a cow to stay cooped up like that. What do I know?

He turned and hobbled off, and I followed him to an outbuilding closest to the road where we stopped and John nodded down at an open space partly graveled but mostly dirt.

"That's where it was before they took off with it."

"Where what was?" I said before I remembered, oh yeah, why he'd called me out there.

"The disk," he said, not adding "dumb ass" although I could tell it was on the tip of his tongue.

"I thought you told me over the phone it was a harrow."

"Rick, a disk *is* a harrow."

Normally a thing like that would embarrass the hell out of me, but his calling me "Rick" had thrown me off because even John would use my name but Trish wouldn't call me anything. After all she'd been to me.

"So what happened, exactly," I said.

"Well, Rick, if I knew what happened *exactly*, I'd go and get my disk back from whoever stole it. Didn't you get the report I made out with Dale Carson?"

Dale is the county sheriff.

"Yeah, it's in the car. Why don't you tell me, though?"

"Well, there's not a hell of a lot to tell. I had it out here because I was working on it, getting it ready to start disking up that bottom land," he said, jerking his thumb over his shoulder. "It was still there this morning when Trish and I ran into Marseilles to the assessor's office. She had a little shopping to do, too. We were gone a couple of hours, back by ten. The disk was gone when we got back."

I eyed the blacktop road. "So they hooked her up behind a tractor and just drove off down the road with her?"

John spat. "Shit. Don't be stupid. They put it on a flatbed."

I felt myself blushing. In some circles around here, being stupid about farm stuff calls your manhood into question.

"I've been working a lot of years, and I've never seen a disk stolen before."

"Well, congratulations. You just busted your cherry."

I don't know why he hates me so. I just don't understand it.

After I'd gotten the call from John about the theft around noon-time, I'd gone online and looked up some stuff about harrows—yeah, now I remember, they are called disks—so I wouldn't appear as ignorant as I really am. "Just by coincidence I was in at the co-op a week or so ago," I lied, "and old Olin Breckenridge, I believe it was—no, maybe not Olin, somebody, though—said he had a disk for sale. Said he wanted five thousand for it."

John cocked his head. "You telling me you think my disk is worth five thousand dollars?"

Uh oh. Had I stepped in it? Maybe he'd been about to tell me his was worth three thousand.

"I don't know anything about yours, John."

"It's all in the sheriff's report."

"The one that's in my car, you mean? Yeah, I'll get around to reading that sometime."

"You always were a wiseass son of a bitch," he said.

But I wasn't. I've always gotten along with people. And John Epps had been my number one or two best friend. What the hell.

"What kind of disk was Orin or whoever it was selling?" John said.

"John Deere. I don't remember what specific model."

John snorted. "That explains it. I wouldn't have a John Deere on my property."

"Yours was a...?"

"International Harvester, of course. And it was worth a hell of a lot more than five thousand dollars. It was worth fifteen if a nickel. It's all in the report."

"Guess I'd better go read that report."

"Guess you had."

These farmers get serious about their equipment. Back in high school I'd seen fights between John Deere kids and I.H. kids. A city person would think it was a strange thing, I guess, but everybody's got something. It just all comes down to where the heart leads you, like the heart led John and Trish to becoming virtual hermits out on a farm only three miles from where we all went to high school together. And like it led me back out there after sundown that same night, flashlight in one hand (although I was afraid to put it on) and one-iron in the other in case I came across some animal I couldn't outrun.

It hadn't occurred to me to go back out to John Epps's farm until supper, which I had at my mother's house. My wife waited until the kids were grown and then she moved out on me. No surprise to anybody. We all knew it was coming. We're still friends, which is pretty much all we ever were. A man only has one true love in his life, and I'm sorry for it, Debbie, but you weren't mine.

Anyway, I was having supper with Ma, telling her about my day, and all of a sudden I heard myself saying, "That disk's still out there on John Epps's farm."

"You think so?"

"I know so," I said although until right then I hadn't thought any such thing. Maybe it had been something that had been sort of stewing in the back of my mind, recalling Terry Pfeiffer saying that John was hell for the dollar, then me being a farm insurance agent for the best part of forty years and never hearing of a disk being stolen. Now I know folks'll steal anything not nailed down, but a disk is a cumbersome thing, hard to move, used worth a few thousand dollars and not half that stolen, I'd bet. Not hardly worth the aggravation. Get an insurance settlement, though, and still have the disk to use—hidden somewhere on the farm—not a bad deal, that.

"What are you going to do?" Ma asked, and I said, "Go back out there and look for it." Nobody could have been more surprised to hear it than me.

I parked the car in a turn-out on the blacktop a quarter of a mile from John's farmhouse. I sat there awhile marveling at what a stupid thing I was doing. I'd dealt with plenty of claims over the years I was pretty damn sure were bogus, but I'd never once taken flashlight and one-iron in hand to prove my point. But then I'd never before had a claim filed by the man who married the woman I loved.

I'd known Trish Springer all my life, but I'd never thought anything about her because she was the Baptist preacher's daughter, and I thought preachers were a different breed of human being, and so their daughters must be, too. She was a year younger than me, which means a lot when you're a kid, and she was a mousy little thing, even shier than I was, so I just never thought a thing about her. Then one summer night there was an ice-cream social out on the Baptist Church parking lot, and my family went even though we were Methodists. There were colored lights like Christmas lights strung up on poles around the parking lot, and fireflies winking off in the darkness, and the soft summer air when you're that age and think the whole world is there just for you tastes almost as sweet as homemade ice cream. I took my paper plate of ice cream and cake and looked for a place to sit, and there all by herself on the steps leading up to the side door of the church sat Trish Springer, not looking mousy now but so cute I couldn't hardly breathe. I've never been a brave person. The one brave act I ever did

was somehow finding the courage to go sit next to Trish. I don't recall
we said much to each other, but there were stars in her eyes, and colored lights like Christmas lights, and winking fireflies in her eyes. We
ate our ice cream and cake and then dumped our paper plates in the
big trash barrel, and then I took her hand and we walked over toward
the trees between the parking lot and the cemetery, the trees where
the fireflies were. I held her hand and we walked among the trees and
the fireflies. I kissed her on the cheek. I think I must have been ten or
eleven, Trish a year younger. We hadn't hit puberty yet. This wasn't
sex, this was love.

That's basically the whole romance between Trish and me.
When we were in high school, I asked her to go to the homecoming
basketball game with me—just the game because I knew the Reverend
would never let her go to the dance afterward—but she said her daddy
wouldn't let her date yet, so I thought, OK, I'll wait until she's eighteen
or out of high school, whichever, because I could wait for Trish.

Then came the end of our senior year and John and I, best
friends, hiked up to Lookout Rock on Flint Hill one day just for something to do. We laid out on the rock in the sun talking about this and
that—the future, I guess—and then John said, shy-like because all of
us guys, us friends, were shy when it came to the subject of girls, hardly
any of us were dating, John said that he'd asked Trish Springer to go
with him to the spring prom.

"*Trish Springer*," I said, I guess in a way that sounded to John
like I thought she was a real dog or something because John said,
"Hey, Trish isn't bad. She's a cute girl," and I said, "Of course she is."

Of course she is.

A year later they were married but living like two hermits out
on a farm that I was, over forty years later, just about to trespass on,

flashlight I was too scared to switch on in one hand and one-iron you'd hold up in a lightning storm because even God couldn't hit it in the other. Even now, looking back on that night, looking back on the day on Lookout Rock, looking back on that firefly-lit summer evening, I don't understand any of it.

I don't know if he was already out there waiting on me, expecting me, or if he heard my car coming up the road and then the engine go off and came out to investigate, but as I came up between two sheds, John stepped out of the night shadows and said, "Rick, what are you doing here."

I'm proud to say I did manage to control my bowels, but it was a close thing.

"Oh, just looking for my golf ball," I said, holding up the one-iron.

"You think I lied to you about the disk, don't you?" he said, and I said, "Well, John, I have to be honest with you, the thought did cross my mind."

We stared at each other awhile, and then I looked away because those stare-down competitions you have as kids I was never any good at and hadn't improved with age. When I looked back he was still staring at me, not angry so much but a look of hurt in his eyes. Then when he finally broke the silence he really threw me for a loop because he said the very thing I'd been thinking, what I should have said: "Rick, what have you got against me? What did I ever do to you?"

"I don't have anything against you, John," I said. And I don't. Never did. Sure, I'm human, and it hurt like hell when he took Trish to the prom, then married her. But I never felt any sense of betrayal because I never told him about how I felt about her. Never told anybody.

That was a secret between me and Trish. Now I'm not so sure Trish was in on it.

"Then why was I cut out?" John said. "Why was I in, then at the last minute I was out, out by myself, on my own?"

I just shook my head. What was he talking about? That's exactly what I asked him: "John, what in the hell are you talking about?"

"You know. Don't pretend. I was a Musketeer just like everybody else. Then you all were gone and I was on my own, out of it. You know damn good and well what I'm talking about. Kid Day."

"Kid—?"

Then it came to me, came to me a little bit at a time because it was so long ago. May, 1968, the last day of classes before high school graduation. Some folks called it Kid Day and some Senior Skip Day because although technically we were supposed to be in class, it was a tradition that the seniors would skip school and dress up some half-ass way, like cowboys or in diapers, some guys in dresses, ride around town throwing water balloons and lighting firecrackers, stuff like that. There were five of us buddies, the Five Musketeers we called ourselves. Clever, hey?

I don't really remember much of what we did Kid Day, but I do recall we met after school the afternoon before, and Larry Utley said we should spend the night out in his granddad's barn, sleep on the hay, have a big ol' time. Only John wasn't there at that moment—late getting out of class or something—and when somebody asked where he was, I said, "Aw, he's off with his lady love someplace. He's got better things to do." I swear I didn't say it to be mean or cut him out but because I really meant it. I would rather have been with Trish Springer than with that bunch of sad sacks, I'll tell you that. Anyway, we took off without him, ate burgers at Y'All Come Inn for supper, and then headed out to Virgil Utley's barn. Harold Miner brought a six-pack of Hamm's. It was the first beer I'd ever drunk. Tried to drink. I got through half of one. Harold finished mine, in fact drank most of that six-pack because none of the rest of us were drinkers and Harold apparently wasn't much of one either because before the night was over he vomited up his beer and hamburger, too. When I think of Kid Day, 1968, I think of the smell of beer-vomit on fresh hay.

John hadn't missed much, it seemed to me, but apparently that wasn't what he thought from the look on his face.

Surely, come on, surely that wasn't what did it—turned an aw-shucks nice guy like John Epps into a virtual hermit, poisoned him on everything in the world except Trish, and then he'd poisoned her against the world, too. Or at least against me. And all because he'd missed out on Kid Day? No, no, no. Explanations for a life can't be that simple. Can't be that stupid. Or maybe there just can't be explanations at all, not where the heart comes in. The heart catches fire, and it burns, and the less sense it makes the hotter it burns.

We just stared at each other. There was the full moon in his eyes, making him look like a crazy man. That same moon was in mine, too, I guess.

I was in my office the next morning with John Epps's papers on the desk in front of me about ready to sign off on the thing when the phone rang. She didn't call me Ricky this time, either.

"You're not going to stop until you find that disk, are you." She said it like a statement not a question, like I was Sherlock Holmes or something and once I got hold of a case I'd shake it like a dog shaking a blacksnake until it was dead at its feet. In fact, just about the last thing on my mind had been going out to look for that disk again, but because it was Trish on the phone, everything changed.

"I suspect not," I said.

I could hear her sigh. "OK, then. You might as well come on out and get this over with. Come on out right now. Before John gets back."

I said OK. I was surprised I could make it sound as calm as I did.

I drove out there and parked off to the side of the blacktop where I had the night before—in case John returned early, I suppose; I don't know what I was thinking—and walked up the road to the farmhouse. Trish was standing outside the front door waiting for me.

"I guess you aren't going to give up until you find it, are you," she said again, like she needed confirmation before proceeding.

"I guess not."

"It's just that he needs the money. You know what beef prices have been doing. Hogs, too."

"It's the anti-red-meat crowd," I said. She nodded.

We walked across the farm lot, then she opened a gate to the pasture and followed me through and closed the gate, and we walked on across the pasture. We didn't say a word to each other. Sometimes I'd let her get a step ahead of me so I could look at her out of the corner of my eye. Closing in on sixty now. Looks it. So what? Oh love, love, love.

We had to climb through the fence on the east side of the pasture, Trish holding the wire up for me because I guess she figured I didn't even know how to do that on a farm. Then the ground rose a bit and then fell toward a copse of trees with a big cottonwood on one end, and beyond the cottonwood there was a deep cut into the earth, erosion or a natural gully, I don't know, but the end of the gully closest to the cottonwood was filled with brush.

"It's down under that," Trish said as we stood on the edge of the gully looking down. "The disk."

"I can't see it."

"John pushed a lot of brush off onto it. He used a blade on the I.H."

"Yeah, it would have taken something like that," I said like I knew what I was talking about. I squinted down into the brush another minute and then said, "Well, I'm going to have to get down into that and see if I can identify the disk. But it's only so the company won't be liable for the loss. That's my job. I won't turn John over to the law, though, Trish."

She didn't say anything.

I climbed down and started pulling limbs and branches away. I'd thought it was a pleasant morning, but it was hot work under the sun. It'd been an unusually dry spring, and soon the air was filled with dust from me slinging that dead brush around, and I was sneezing and sweating. I don't know how long I was at it. I'd dug down deep enough that that the level of the brush around me was above my head in places. I could finally catch a glimpse of something metallic gleaming down under the brush but couldn't tell for sure what it was. I was hot, beat.

I was already to say, There she is, the disk, I see it, even though I hadn't for sure seen it when I heard a sound like something splashing above me, and then there was a *whoosh* and a bright light, and even though I was looking at it all around me I swear until I smelled it I didn't realize it was fire.

I started clawing at the brush, trying to fight my way out of there, throwing branches left and right, coughing, cussing, screaming, took me ten minutes it seemed like although it couldn't possibly have been more than a few seconds or that fire would have got me for sure.

Then somehow I was to the bank of the gully, half-running half-crawling up the crumbly side, blinded by the smoke, coughing, choking, then up out of the gully with the fire safely behind me but still terrified because I knew John had to be out there waiting to go upside my head with a spade or gut me with a corn knife or just blow me to kingdom come with a double-barrel, I wouldn't put anything past somebody who'd toss kerosene at a man and try to set him on fire.

I just ran, ran as fast as a totally-exhausted coughing wheezing half-blinded sixty-year-old could run. I ran across the pasture. My vision cleared enough that I saw cows on the west side of the pasture next to the road, where I was headed. I was too scared of John to be afraid of them. "Out of my way, you sons of bitches!" I hollered, and those cows moved fast, like I was the scariest sight they'd seen in many a day.

I climbed through the fence, didn't need anybody to hold the wire for me. Got in my car and started it up and did a U-turn and barreled down the road away from John Epps's farm. I was a menace behind the wheel, eyes still smarting and teary from the smoke, but I could see well enough that, a mile or so on down the road, I saw John in his pickup, that horse trailer behind it, pass me going the other way. Coming back from the auction. Then I finally figured out who set the fire. Anybody else would have known it from the get-go. Anybody not blinded by smoke and dust and fireflies.

Most folks around here call them lightning bugs. I call them fireflies because that summer night—it must have been 1959, 1960, around then—when I took Trish's hand but didn't know what to do next, she said to me, "Let's go walk among the fireflies, Ricky." I think it was the way she said "among the fireflies"—that's when I fell in love with her.

My earliest memories of fireflies were when I was a very little boy out in the back yard with my older sister, Fayrene, chasing lightning bugs, she called them. Fayrene caught one and pinched off its light and came at me with it, saying, "It's gonna burn you, gonna burn!"

I just stood there because I couldn't believe my older sister, whom I adored, would hurt me. But then she grabbed my wrist and I started to send up a howl before she stuck the light on my finger and said, "There, you got you a wedding ring." Oh, how beautiful. But then it began to fade, and I ran after Fayrene, pleading, "Burn me, sis, burn me."

Like they say, be careful what you wish for.

Wychwood Park

James Deahl

After a painting by Mary Hiester Reid

Near dusk a November sky
dips its hands into the pond.
Nightbirds hide among pale reeds;
the first parlour lights switch on.

The silence of the world surrounds you
as your shadow stands in water.
Ripples move, spread, decline.
Night is the only philosopher—

your living blood the only warmth
as air and earth embrace.

Breakfast on the Road

Although spring is close
winter has soaked into the land
and is too stubborn to leave.
A silver sky holds the memory
of snow. The diner windows
are ghosted with steam,
every tune on the juke box
at least twenty-five years old.
Why worry about my poverty?
I eat homefries and sausage
in the red-brick morning,
lay plans to visit Hartford later.

The abandoned canal reminds
of more prosperous times;
some of these buildings must go back
to early mercantile days, to what
we want to imagine was a period
of innocence, and long for.
I sit drinking a second coffee
in Plainville, Connecticut

while listening to Ray Charles,
mechanics from the service station
two booths away, when the sun
breaks through like luck.

Regions of the Heart

O silence, golden zero
Unsetting sun

Love winter when the plant says nothing.

— Thomas Merton

We enter the last month of snow.
The sun hangs in its black locust,
dried quinces in their skeletal hedge.

Cold winds rattle cattails where marsh
meets lake. The implacable wheel
continues to turn, every season

returning to its winter roots,
to its wells of solitude.
Because we begin in error

and at the solstice of unknowing,
our sun so far removed, we end
in these stark, white fields of longing.

Slowly the crows commence returning.
Even our starlings, beaten south
by January's storms, are back.

But the birds, also, travel through
unknown regions of the heart.
We reach life's dark abyss.

Every struggle has driven us
to this blessèd anguish.
An immaculate silence,

a ledge as thin as air,
far below either death or love
and no way back.

*

Simon Perchik

To warm this grave its wick
is lit the way a small stone
ignites the Earth with footsteps

brought here to become the glow
dirt breathes in, half harvest
half let go and though the night sky

no longer makes room
it still thickens—you gather
as if all stones are emptied

for their canary-in-the-mine wind
darkness alone can calm, turn back
and your arm at last on its side

folded over the other :ice
headed for winter, filled
without a past, without faces.

Anti-Anxiety Pill

Sara Kirschenbaum

My two kids and I are visiting my parents back east in New York City, where I grew up. Taking my five-year-old son, Sage, and nearly-two-year-old daughter, Annie, on the plane is no easy task. Their father had to stay home and work. Five and a half hours is a long time for them to sit in their seats. When we finally arrive and I put them to bed in my old room, I realize that single parenting is heroic. And it seems to me, untenable in the long run. My patience is wearing thin and my aging parents are less helpful than I imagined they'd be.

Bringing my kids into my childhood home feels sweet but also psychologically treacherous. I find myself wary and judgmental around my parents. They both still drink a lot and my father fights his depression by yelling and railing at my mother. My obsessive-compulsive disorder is flaring up and I am overcome with intrusive images of horrible accidents. I'm afraid that if I don't do penance in the form of embarrassing and pointless rituals the disasters will come true; I seek comfort and protection in lining up cutlery and other objects in neat lines. At least I am not having one of those stumble-out-of-bed-and-gag panic attacks. Instead, it is a long, slow one that goes on for days. It is a panic attack that, with effort, I can hide from others. I am freaking out, politely, from the inside out. The sweat breaks out on my skin and radiates through my shirt and wool sweater, until I smell like a dirty frightened sheep in heat.

I hate these days-long bouts of mental illness. But there is a solution—an easy, reliable solution. It's orange. It's round. It has the words "KLONOPIN ROCHE" stamped into it. It is my "anti-anxiety" pill. But whenever I approach the bottle that I'm carrying around with me on this vacation, I am visited by my conscience. No, make that two consciences. And oh, what a racket.

Cartoons show a little red devil in a red suit whispering in one ear and an angel in a white dress whispering in the other. My consciences' personas aren't clearly good or evil—that would make choosing easier—but they do have their own ways of looking at the world. Flying above one ear, on one side of my head, is the tiny figure of my stalwart psychiatrist from Boston, Dr. Sichel. She is a strong woman in a navy wool skirt, white shirt, and flowery green scarf. She stamps her miniature navy blue pumps in the air. She is opinionated, compassionate and brilliant, and shouts in my ear. She hovers with translucent wings. Over the other hemisphere, just above my other ear, is a composite of every new age therapist or peer counselor to whom I've ever spilled my guts to in Portland, my adopted home. This conscience wears a black and white batik dress, and smells vaguely of patchouli essential oil. She is in her purple house slippers. Her voice is lilting and dreamy. She has an unshakable conviction that I can heal myself. Her wings are violet. Together my consciences flap their wings and lower themselves to speak directly into each ear.

Sara, Sara, Sara. Don't run away from your feelings. Do I have to remind you again of the Rilke quote, "Why do you want to shut out of your life any agitation, any pain, any melancholy?... Since you know that you are in the midst of transitions and wished for nothing so much as change." Sara, honey, there is no way around but through.

> Don't think so. It doesn't make you a better person to suffer. It just makes you tired. Your liberation, Sara, is in your acceptance of *relief.*

What a wonderful opportunity you have to work through another layer of your childhood hurt! If you numb yourself up with drugs, you will lose this chance. Don't you think it's interesting that you have not told your parents how you are feeling on this trip and they have not seemed to notice? Do you think this is normal? How do you think that felt as a child?

> Pop a Klonopin! It is metabolized quickly—it will be out of your system in a day. It's a chemical solution to a chemical problem.

You're strong, Sara. You can do it. There are only five more days until you go home and then I'm sure it will be easier. Won't you be proud to go home with all ten Klonopins still in your fannypack?

> If a diabetic needs insulin, they should have it. So you have impaired neurotransmitter receptors and you need a Klonopin. Just because you are good at hiding the pain doesn't mean it isn't real pain. Just because the defective part is in your brain, doesn't mean it doesn't deserve fixing. I can help you.

Sara, answer me one thing. I'm going to ask you a question and you tell me the first thing that comes to mind. Who did this to you? Who hurt you in this way? There *is* a reason you feel like this. What did they do to you?

So, I am in New York City, where I grew up. I have nine and a half little orange Klonopins with me. I am crossing the street with my father, and my kids. We are on our way to the Lower East Side Tenement Museum to learn how my grandparents lived. The half-Klonopin streams through my arteries, putting out a thousand fires. Every part of my body feels calmer, though much of me thinks I cheated. The half-pill blossoms its chemicals into my veins, comforting me with a slurry of cashmere and chamomile. I begin to land in the present moment, on the sidewalk, without the forward and back time machines of fear and second guessing. I begin to notice where I am right now—Chinatown—without the self-consciousness of my panic. Looking out, I see the bluish and red crabs in wooden baskets at the fish stores. Bushels of lychee nuts are still wrapped in their leathery pink-brown shells. My daughter's tiny hand tugs at mine. She wants, more than anything in the whole wide world, a fuzzy mechanical parrot that chirps a song if you clap your hands. Five of these parrots are hanging from the street seller's shopping cart, constantly chirping, bobbing, and twitching their tails. In a chaotic musical round they sing London Bridge Is Falling Down, Beethoven's Ninth Symphony, and Oh, What a Beautiful Morning. We buy the pink one and carry it with us, chirping, to the Tenement Museum on the Lower East Side.

About a dozen people are gathered to go on the Tenement Museum tour. Many of them, like us, are relatives of people who grew up in this neighborhood. The interpretive guide at the Tenement Museum takes us to the dim stairwell of the museum. This tenement was boarded up in 1935 and so most things are unchanged since then, as if in a time capsule. In a few of the apartments, they've recreated the furnishings of specific families who lived in those very rooms.

The walls in the stairwell are filthy with coal and wood dust. The guide points out that under the dust are quite lovely pastoral paintings painted when gas lamps were first added to the hallway. "Imagine," says the guide, "what it was like before they put in these small gas lamps. There was total darkness. Imagine that every time you needed to go the bathroom you had to walk through these dark halls to the outhouse in the backyard."

Annie is holding the parrot in one hand and my father's hand in the other. We head up to an apartment that they have fixed up to look like it did in 1918—six years before my father was born. Sage, my earnest son with the long blond hair, walks a few steps ahead of us. When we step into the apartment, we see three neat, modest rooms. There is worn linoleum on the floor, and a few pieces of wood furniture. My father says, "This is just what your grandfather father had when he was growing up. This is it exactly. Can you imagine, nine or more people living in these three rooms? In my dad's family there were both parents, six kids, and usually a couple of boarders."

Sage looks up to his grandfather reverently. Annie plays with the pink feathery tail of her mechanical parrot that she has reluctantly turned off.

The apartment is fixed up to look as it did when the Rogarshevskys were sitting Shiva, in mourning for their father who died of Tuberculosis in this very apartment. In keeping with Jewish custom for grieving, the mirror is covered by a cloth; the table has several plates of round foods like bagels, oranges and eggs. I can't imagine how I would have managed my OCD 90 years ago in this tiny stuffy dark three room apartment with eight or ten people living (and dying) here.

There is a vague story in our family about one of my father's aunts going crazy after being traumatized in a botched robbery. The aunt evidently spent the rest of her days in an insane asylum. I've also recently learned that my father's father "kind of lost it" when my dad was fighting in the Second World War. My grandfather had to "go away" to some kind of resort to recuperate. I don't know how people with mental illnesses survived back then – heck, I can't even imagine how I'd get along *today* without the flowering calm of my half Klonopin.

After our tour in the Tenement Museum, we go have blintzes at Ratner's—a famous dairy restaurant on the Lower East Side that my relatives undoubtedly visited. Annie gets blueberry blintzes and Sage, my dad, and I get strawberry. I take out a tape recorder to record my father telling stories about his father growing up on the Lower East Side. But half a sentence in, the tape recorder jams. We head home full of the cheesy blintzes and fruit. We catch a bus on Third Avenue and head home with the pink parrot chirping and the kids churning restlessly, and joyfully, in the molded plastic seats.

Hippie conscience pouts; psychiatrist gloats.

Each Hour, Each Mile

R.T. Castleberry

Sleeping mean, I wake when I want,
a broken comb, a drugstore watch
tumbling to the bedroom floor.
A high rise searchlight races
freeway cars towards
mistress hotel or microwave meal.
A quarter moon wind fractures fog, mist,
rumble of overpass and passing horns.
I consider the cost of bitterness and battle,
the familiar line of debt, implied or specific.
I repeat my emotions,
the practical stance from 1980, from 1987.
I remove myself from consideration,
change my address, my inflection at will.
In the warring day,
a bullet-broken window shatters in its frame.
I send my children east.

Sweet Victory

M.E. Mitchell

It wasn't funny anymore. All their snide remarks about my limp had
worn thin and I couldn't find an ounce of humor in what my cowork-
ers considered harmless fun. Granted, I said nothing when the subtle
digs began during their first week on the job, but now, three months
later, the gag was still going strong. Perhaps my quiet demeanor sig-
naled I was a willing target, or my smile a consenting nod for their
acrid jokes. Enough was enough and I should have blasted my tormen-
tors the first time the word *gimp* was flung in my face.

Grooms Zack and Tully leaned against the railing of the open-
air barn, pointing and laughing as they smoked their cigarettes. I plod-
ded through the deep sand of the walking ring, which emphasized my
ailment even more, and I felt as though I was parading naked before
them. At times I thought I spotted the makings of a good horsemen in
these novices, but my attempts to instruct them were met with shrugging
shoulders and a "Who cares?" attitude. So I stopped offering years of
knowledge to this indifferent audience and reasoned it was better to keep
silent. The slow meticulous process by which I had learned my craft did
not apply to these fools; their philosophy was to do the work without
much effort, get paid, then bolt out the door to bet the Daily Double. The
boss' much too liberal nature made it easy for them to oil their way into
his confidences, which made the rest of us on the shed wonder how he
ever got to train forty plus head of horses in the first place. Damn, if only

he hadn't told me to cool out Victory for Rome after a late morning gallop, my work would have been finished and I'd be back in the solitude of my dormitory room finishing that paperback I picked up at the bodega.

No one had made me so conscious of my awkward gait before. In this line of work, furious kicks received from startled thoroughbreds eventually take their toll on a body, not to mention a seven-day work-week with the occasional Sunday off. This leg of mine had endured much, but then I knew what I was getting into back in '73 when I announced to astonished family and friends that I had chosen the racetrack over college. I hung around the stable gate hoping trainers driving onto the grounds would stop and say they had work for me. All through the summer and autumn, disinterested eyes either stared straight ahead or gazed with vulgar intent. I countered the offers that had nothing to do with equine care with a polite "Not me" and resumed my vigil on the steps outside the Pinkertons' office. If no job surfaced by the end of the year, I promised myself I would hop any van heading south and check out the Ocala horse farms. Thankfully, someone spared me an uncomfortable ride down I-95.

"Hey!" A male voice shattered that quiet Christmas dawn. "Know how to handle a pitchfork?"

I sprinted through the piles of snow, and slipped on an ice patch which landed me at the feet of a small, rather scraggly individual with bits of hay and straw dust clinging to his coat. The man peered at me through grimy spectacles as I rose to my feet unassisted.

"I worked at a riding academy during high school." My reply came off sounding like a shameless boast.

"Well, I'm running a racing stable, not a riding academy," he snapped. "Or at least I'm trying to. Say, you aren't one of them women libbers? Because if you are, I can't use you."

His manner, as well as his appearance, put me off and I turned to leave.

"Look, I'm sorry," he said, removing his cap which revealed a mass of matted, gray curls. "I hoped to spend Christmas with the family, but I got a shed full of horses and no help. You got a job, if you want."

"Really?"

"Yes, really. Come on, we've got a lot of mucking out to do."

He walked into the barn and I followed without any further questions or qualms, all those arduous, precious years ago.

"Hey, mama!" Tully shouted as I stopped to catch my breath. "Need some crutches?"

"That won't help," Zack added. "More likely she could use one of those electric wheelchairs to buzz around in. Just tie the horse to it and she's got it made."

I ignored the remarks and quickened my pace, hoping somehow that would miraculously make my limp invisible. This brilliant maneuver only increased the agony in my knee and forced me to halt again, but Victory for Rome grew impatient with the inactivity and rubbed his head hard against my jacket. He pranced a few steps ahead of me on the shank, then eyed me as if to say, "Well, are you coming?" I whispered a tired "All right, Vic" and continued our walk.

Zack hobbled about, imitating my malady as his friend hooted and cackled with inane glee. God help me, I still had ten minutes left before I could return the horse to his stall and hightail it away from this place. I fought the impulse to launch a verbal assault, since screaming like a fishwife would be unwise alongside such a fractious and expensive two-year old. So I made mental notes of the choice expletives I would hurl at them later, away from the workplace, and imagined their pea brains unable to handle my merciless offense. But these were fanciful images never meant for reality, for I knew too well, the coward in me had grown deep, comfortable roots.

A warm breeze stirred the leaves of the palms towering over the barn as an aphotic hue enveloped the sky. At first, soft droplets fell, but while hurrying the colt toward the stable, the drizzle had become a downpour. The fronds of the palmetto trees crackled harshly from the pummeling rain, making Victory for Rome buck and neigh as we darted into the stable. I tried to calm his agitation with reassuring pats on his shoulder, but my own uneasiness heightened upon seeing my antagonists waiting ahead with toothy grins. Our boss had apparently slipped away to the backstretch kitchen before the cloudburst and was undoubtedly enjoying a cup of coffee while the Florida heavens battered the area. I would prefer a soaking in the deluge than being stuck indoors with Tully and Zack, but the storm had already turned the walking ring into a mud pool.

The heavy rain failed to alleviate the humidity. With one hand free and the other on the shank, I struggled to remove my jacket, but the wet material clung to my skin. I cursed myself for the difficulty I was having with what should have been a simple task. Impatient Victory for Rome pounded the dirt with his hoof.

Zack approached. "Let me help, old girl" he said and tugged at the obstinate sleeve.

I numbly complied despite the warning bells clamoring in my head. He threw the jacket aside and clamped his hand on my shoulder.

"What's your hurry?" Tully chimed in. "Hell, lame or old, doesn't make any difference to us."

"I...I have to finish," I replied, my words barely audible.

Zack's fingers dug into my skin. "Time ain't been very good to you, gimp," he laughed. "Maybe you could use some action. A little bit on the side...who's to know?"

I snapped out of my daze and shook free of his grip. The colt lurched forward, dragging me with him. Despite the jolt to my leg, I was grateful for the almost intuitive move my companion had made. His massive strides lengthened and quickened to a frantic clip as we made our way toward the corner of the barn. My efforts to slow him went unheeded. He snorted and danced about sideways, delighting in the fact that he was in complete control now. Blackness had descended across the backstretch as gusts of wind tore through the shed, along with a churning invasion of broken branches and trash. My trembling pleas to stop became lost amidst the tumult. Dust and debris clouded my vision. Even in his frenzied state, I had to rely on Victory for Rome to guide my steps. My hands ached from hanging onto the lead, my legs buckled from exhaustion, yet we had made it to the other side of the barn. The horse abruptly stopped when two figures emerged from the shadows. I fell against his pulsating body and struggled for breath.

I gasped, "When the boss finds out—"

"Nothing," Tully interrupted. "He won't find out nothing."

He reached for the shank, but I let it drop to the ground. As Zack went to retrieve it, the horse reared and came down on his arm, the sharp hooves ripping a deep gash in his skin.

"Damn!" He cried, trying to stop the bleeding with his bandanna. "I'll kill that no-count piece of shit!"

Victory for Rome's nostrils flared, savoring the scent of the damage he had inflicted. My body shook uncontrollably as I steered the horse past the men. By now, Tully's whining had taken on histrionic proportions. His associate propped him against the wall, then rushed toward me.

"It's not finished!" Zack shouted, striking me in the back with his fist.

Victory for Rome released a piercing squeal and with teeth bared, lunged at my assailant who toppled back into a row of stacked hay. The colt circled about as I clung to the end of the shank. He was a wild, primitive thing, bucking and rearing, clearly relishing every moment of this unrestrained behavior. In spite of my feeble efforts to settle him, I admired his spirit, applauded his dance of freedom—he was magnificent.

Zack struggled to regain his footing. With pinpoint accuracy, the colt let loose one swift kick which connected with the groom's leg. I heard the sharp crack, heard the guttural moans from the crumpled body on the ground and felt no remorse. Perhaps I would be calling *him* gimp now. As far as I was concerned, those two lowlifes were victims of their own misconduct.

The horse ceased his tirade. Once again docile, he nudged me to move on. The rain and winds slowly subsided. I led my comrade to his stall, made sure he had settled in, then phoned security from the boss' office. I bolted the door and waited. Something I had been reading the previous night popped into my head.

All sorts of things occur to help one that never otherwise would have occurred.

Not sure if it was Goethe. When I'd get back to my room, I'd have to find that page again.

Voices of Schizophrenia

Connie Post

There are birds
I will bring
that will fly crooked
in the bent sky

their feathers are matted
with the screaming spit
of the gods

they have flown here
from a foreign land
to tell you

all those times
they landed
on the sacred lake
of sanity

were never
for you

Not Like the Rest

I have never had a pedicure
I do not want anyone else
hovering around my feet
—to come close enough
to smell the blood I have walked upon
from the roads of centuries passed
I am too afraid, they will find
ancient bone fragments between my toes,
realize I am not from this time

I imagine their solemn faces
pretending I am like the rest
asking me about my children's ages
or, if I will get my hair done tomorrow
I will look away
as they slowly understand
that my hair is coated with the marrow
of other wars
my skin has been nailed shut with
the thorns of a burnt rose bush

I keep my feet covered
pull them away from the clamor
of absolved hands
I go to bed at night and feel soldiers
rise and fall beneath my bed
they eventually lie silent, as do I
but each morning
I wake to hot coals
placed in distinct lines across
the floor of my bedroom

I avoid them
on the way to the shower
but traveling back
I fall—and later must explain
to the mute man at the grocery counter
why my hands
are burned beyond recognition

Fire Line

The fire starts like a bad conversation
spreading through wilderness
jumping from one tree to another

people watch from miles away
the smoke rising
like sin from a body

weeks later
the charred earth remains
like a welt on the land

eventually the soil understands
the language of submission
how to stay quiet when night comes

planes will fly overhead
noticing the edges of black
—how a loss is contained

as summer leaves
the fields seem to heal

Fire Line

the deepest green seeps to the surface
like old discolored blood from a bruise

everyone is quiet for a while
months pass
everyone forgets
drives by the quiet hills
as if they are redeemed

then in fall
the rain begins
continues on and on
like a story without chapters

how easily a mud slide happens
how easily a mind succumbs

and when they come to look for you
they will have to move
the granules of earth aside
with their bare and swollen hands

Where I Live, and Why I Moved Here

William Jolliff

Some folks you know are better company
from a distance. You can entertain pride
in the wonders of kin, safe in the fact
that sea-to-shining-sea is five days by car.

Like heavenly bodies or British food,
some good attributes are clearest when viewed
from far above the surface, say *orbit*,
safely adrift in the silence of space.

The Lilliputians, Gulliver discovered,
were so pearline in countenance because
size did for them what distance can sometimes
do for those less blessedly small: it shrinks

our faults and lets our basic human shape
overcome our irregularities.
So the homefolks were less distraught than you
might have thought when I took off for Oregon.

In My Life with Carl Lehmann

Joseph Holt

Trevor Thomas was like me! We were classmates, neighbors, A-one buddies. From the start we got on famously: we spotted each other across an intersection wearing the same print of flannel shirt, both tucked into our blue jeans. He was the wind and I was the chime that rattled, I the flint and he the tinder that caught spark. Me and him, the two of us—we were plain simpatico.

Those days I leased a narrow, jerry-built A-frame in the Mission District of San Francisco, and Trevor Thomas rented an attic across the alleyway. With his mile-a-minute strides, he could reach my front door in seconds. He might barge in to discuss an assignment of ours at the Art Institute. Or, more likely, he wanted to pace my living room and jabber-jaw about his latest grand idea, his hands cutting swaths through the air and his eyes agog into perfect rings of white.

He was a jack-of-all-trades, picking up woodcutting, collage, photography—anything that struck his fancy. But his passion was lithography. Once, when I confessed that I could hardly pronounce the word, let alone comprehend the lithographic process, he gave me a stirring pep talk on zinc and ink. His idea wasn't to instruct me, but just to share his enthusiasm. Trevor Thomas could turn anyone into a believer, like he did for me with Minty Coke.

One afternoon he stormed through my door with a paper bag from the 7-Eleven and shoved a folder in my hands marked MINTY

COKE BUSINESS PROPOSAL. Then he disappeared into the kitchen, where he popped open soda cans and clanged together ceramic mugs.

I sat on my loveseat leafing through the proposal—fifteen pages of various florae sketched in colored pencil. In time I joined him and returned the proposal, which he stuffed into the empty paper bag.

"Forget that," he said. "It's time for the blind taste test."

He swept his arm toward four mugs on the countertop, unveiling them like a game show host. In front of each mug was a card—A, B, C, and D—made on construction paper with glitter and Elmer's glue.

"You're in for a treat, old boy." He straightened the cards and arranged the handles of the mugs. "Ready? You can start with A."

Such spectacle was common for Trevor Thomas. I reached out and gulped from the A mug. "Good job." I let out a little burp and smiled. "That tasted like Coca-Cola."

"It is Coca-Cola," he said. "But that's not the point. For now, just remember that mug was good, but not the best." He plunged his hands into his pockets and shifted his weight underfoot, creaking the floorboards. "There's three more."

I tried the mug for B. It was Tab.

"Halfway," said Trevor Thomas. His face took on a look of painful concentration. "About those first two sodas: they're pretty good, right? But how could they taste even better? Something's missing—something new, something fresh."

"I wanna keep going," I interrupted. "I like this!" With his permission I took up the C mug: root beer, my favorite. "That one's the best," I told Trevor Thomas. "That's my vote."

"You haven't tried them all." He pointed at D, another dark soda, this one with an oily sheen floating at the top. "Drink the final mug."

D tasted sharp and spicy, almost hot. It made me cough. My eyes watered and my throat burned, and a glob of something stuck in my gullet. I tried hawking up, but that gave me the nasal drip.

"Now, which one do you think contains a tablespoon of Vicks Vapo-Rub?"

I wiped my nose on my sleeve. "Number D," I said.

"Well. You are..." He paused for dramatics. "Correct! It's D, Carl. You're the first fan of Minty Coke!"

"I knew it! I could tell when the menthol hit my throat."

"Good work, my friend." He drank from the other side of the D mug. He winced. "Still a prototype. But you won the taste test, and Minty Coke won, too. We're all winners, Carl! Let's make a toast— champagne all around. You don't have champagne, do you?"

I shook my head no. My cupboards were constantly empty in those days.

"Drink the D," I told him. And we toasted one another, him with the Minty Coke and me with the root beer.

After we'd finished the colas and were left standing around my kitchen, just smiling and feeling good, Trevor Thomas picked up the vial of craft-store glitter he'd used for the lettered signs. He held it up to the light, as if it was a science-class test tube. I could tell the wheels were turning.

"I wonder if you could put glitter in Minty Coke," he said, more to himself than to me. "Shoot. Now I hafta rewrite that whole proposal."

"That's the burden of genius," I said.

But the lithographs—there was genius! Of all his lithographs, the one I remember best was Willie Mays in his batting stance, an image Trevor Thomas copied from an old baseball card. He used that image for his Bring Mays Back campaign, the idea of which was to spur

Willie Mays out of retirement. Using stationery pilfered from the Institute, he produced a series of 8½"x11" goldenrod fliers which he stapled to every tree and light post within the Fell and Oak Streets Panhandle.

Eventually the fliers went missing, faded in the rain, or were defaced with mustaches and googly eyes. Bring Mays Back was, in the end, what you might call an awareness campaign. Trevor Thomas never had much in mind for an endgame. One problem was, the lithographed card dated to Willie Mays's early years, when the Giants were still in New York, and the NY on his cap might have confused people. Another problem: this was the late 1970s and Willie Mays was nearly fifty years old, long retired.

Sometime later we went to a party at some dude's house, where one of the living room walls was pasted with Bring Mays Back fliers. This dude thought himself an art collector and said he adhered to the Dada and Fluxus movements, which didn't mean scratch to me and Trevor Thomas. Just then some bohos waltzed through the room and the dude excused himself.

Trevor Thomas leaned in and investigated the fliers. His eyes went big. "This rocks me," he said. "I could do something like this! I could totally do this. All I'd need is a picture of Willie Mays—I must have an old baseball card lying around somewhere."

I looked closer. My nose tingled: the fliers had been adhered to the wall with rubber cement. I said, "You're the Lithograph King. This almost looks as good as something you would do," because I too had forgotten that Bring Mays Back was Trevor Thomas's creation.

"Hmpf. It's such a pity. It guts me, man. Like all the best ideas are already taken."

I nodded. It was a shame, I felt. It seemed unfair, even, the way Trevor Thomas had said it. For an instant I had a tiny sick feeling in my throat, a feeling I didn't know what to do with. Trevor Thomas felt it too.

"Come on," he sniffled. "Be tough, old boy." He led me out of the living room. He said, "We're letting the rubber cement fumes get the best of us."

One time Trevor Thomas came over with a ream of paper on Friday afternoon, took my typewriter from the closet, and hunkered down at my kitchen table. When I asked his plan, he told me he needed privacy. All that evening I watched television in my living room, and from the kitchen rang the pounding of keys and the recoil of the carriage. You might think the noise bothered me, but I was glad for the company.

Around midnight he joined me on the loveseat, where together we watched Johnny on *The Tonight Show*. Trevor Thomas fidgeted all over his cushion. At last he said, "Would you please go away so I can take a snooze on this couch?"

"What were you making in there?" I asked. But at that moment his head dropped onto the armrest. I pulled his legs up and covered him with my slumber bag, then retreated to the cot-size mattress on the floor of my little bedroom.

He typed throughout the next day, breaking now and again to pace the kitchen and mutter to himself. By evening my stomach was grumbling, and I poked my head in to ask if Trevor Thomas was hungry as well.

"Now that you say something, I believe I'm on the verge of fainting. I would like pizza, and lots of it. Some Coke would be nice too." He stood and pulled several handfuls of coin from his jeans pocket, plunking it all down onto the table. "Use this," he said. "I found it in your couch."

It was the mother lode—over ten dollars! I stretched my shirt into a coin pouch and he scooped it in. Then I nodded toward the stack of pages beside the typewriter. "What's that?"

"Nothing," he said. I tried sneaking a look, but he danced around to block my view. "Patience," he told me. "I ain't done yet."

"I'm curious," I said, peeking over his shoulder. "Won't you read me the first part? Or a portion. Read me the first line—just a single sentence."

"Here's the first line," he said, boxing me out from the typewriter. "'Page one.'"

"Please," I argued. "I'm so curious I could explode. Be a pal."

"Oh, fine," he said and grabbed the top sheet from the stack. He puckered his lips and blurted some nonsense sounds like an actor warming his vocal cords. "Dear *Chronicle* Editor," he intoned. "I am writing in regards to the rumor of a sea monster dwelling in the strait below the Golden Gate Bridge. As a concerned citizen, I would appreciate a full inquiry into this matter. I would especially appreciate a mayoral declaration on whether traversing the bridge is safe under these conditions." He concluded, "Sincerely yours, Albert Peacock, M.D."

"Superb," I told him. "I'd slap you on the back if I wasn't holding all these coins."

"And that's just the beginning," he said, looking down to the stack of typed pages. Around us, even more crumpled sheets lay about the worn linoleum floor. "Buddy, I'm starving. What about that pizza?"

So I was out the door. When I returned, we dined and watched some *CHiPS*. Then he returned to the typewriter, and later I bedded down to the clicking of keys.

The next morning Trevor Thomas yelled from the kitchen, "Fifty! Hot cha!" He stomped into my living room and punched in the power knob of the television. I pulled my legs underneath me on the loveseat. "Okay. Dear *Chronicle* Editor." He began with the Albert Peacock, M.D., letter. And he had more—fifty of them!—all persuading the *Chronicle*'s Editor-in-Chief to investigate what he called the Golden Gate Monster.

"Preliminary estimates cite five heads and twenty mouths," Trevor Thomas read to me. "Local sailors report its scales to be razor sharp, its fangs stronger than titanium." The legend grew with each letter. He wrote that the Golden Gate Monster's eyes were formed of acid fire. Its tail could reach out and strangle all of Oakland. At will, it could transform the bridge's suspension cables into snakes. Already, brigades of the strongest, most valiant men had fallen to its fierce bloodlust. "Must we never cross into Marin County again?" he asked of the *Chronicle*. Letters upon letters now scattered my living room floor. "Please—as organ of our vulnerable city, brandish your pens! The City by the Bay depends upon you!" He looked to me for emphasis. In his hand was the final page. "Most sincerely yours," he concluded, "Timmy Tumbleweed."

Yes! I was nodding my head like I was listening to music. It was monumental! It was what I should have expected from Trevor Thomas.

He sat next to me on the loveseat. "Forty-Niners game on yet?"

I believe it was just starting, and I believe he conked out at the opening kickoff.

I'm trying to think now if any letters got published, or whether the *Chronicle* ever reported on the Golden Gate Monster. It seems like something I'd remember, but I don't. What might have happened was that Trevor Thomas didn't have envelopes or postage, then something else captured his fancy and he plumb forgot.

There were long stretches when I didn't see Trevor Thomas. Our paths at the Institute began to veer apart. Previously I'd dabbled in painting and collage, and sometimes animation or welded sculptures or décollage, and I admit I suffered flights of attention. Eventually I honed in on music composition, for which I spent hours on end in my concrete cellar recording onto my four-track with my bass guitar, Moog and trap set, creating scores and compositions for sine waves and looping reverb. I would lock the front door while I was in my cellar, spending entire weekends down there in complete bliss. So what I'm thinking now is I might have incidentally shut Trevor Thomas out of my life.

To create a composition, I would bend the high string of the bass guitar to its peak, then, at the same speed, lower it to its original position, all the while scraping the length of the string with the dull end of a butter knife. This process would last twelve to twenty seconds depending on my intended duration for the sine wave loop. I would then stomp the looping pedal at a precise microsecond to ensure the wave traveled a naturally full arc. That, in short, would be the basis for a composition, though I would further manipulate the pitch and tone by toggling the dials on my four-track. Then I would add rhythm from the trap set, Moog sound effects (I liked the spaceship roar), and, eventually, an additional bass rhythm. My general goal was to start each track with an uncompounded arrangement, then, as the instrumental layering intensified, make small adjustments to the duration of the sine curve (which by that point would be aurally backgrounded) and modify the trap set rhythm accordingly so that, as the instrumental crescendo approached, the score would transmogrify into a varied and unrecognizable sound pattern, which I would then use as the harmonic basis for my next composition. Sometimes I dropped the butter knife and bungled it all up.

I even cut a tape—*The Best Sogs with Carl Lehmann* (typo my fault)! For a couple years I gigged around the Bay Area, most the time accepting my pay in sandwiches. And once I sold my five-hundredth and final copy of *Best Sogs*, I happily called myself retired.

As I was working on my compositions, I felt I was truly in control. Locking the door was part of that. But also, I knew it wouldn't earn me any money or power, so I could pursue my own vision. Those days in San Francisco, self-indulgence was going at a cut rate. Before my wife entered the picture, music was the self-indulgence that kept my head glued on proper.

My wife—she's everything to me! Her name is Betty!

Betty and me are kindred. We're the best of friends. She's always smiling and I'm happy to please her. Her dark black hair is cut into a bob, and she has a delicate little nose and cheekbones. One time as a prank she disconnected the starter in my Festiva, and under the hood she'd placed a handwritten note saying I was her spark plug. Another time I drew a picture of the stars in a constellation of her, then stuck it with a magnet on our refrigerator. Betty's the object of all my adoration. I could brag about her until my voice escapes me. How's this for a story: I love my wife!

Together we have a house in Halethorpe, Maryland, and a knuckleheaded fourteen year old named Carl Jr. who we enroll in all sorts of clubs and lessons so he doesn't pester us every minute of the day. I'm in the tax accountancy game, and Betty works from home selling hospital supplies to the Greater Baltimore area. Life is constantly wonderful. I couldn't be unhappy if I tried.

Betty and I met at a roadside diner in North Platte, Nebraska, of all places. After I left California I took work on a construction team that erected vinyl-sided storage units. Our team of six moved from town to town, pocketing straight cash. I headed up the framework and bracketing, making sure the angles of the studs and rafters were legit. I got lost in that job, weeks at a time often passing without my notice.

In North Platte we blew the whistle at sundown and headed to the diner where Betty waited tables. Immediately I was keen on her, for she was a doll and a top-notch waitress to boot. When I would special order my burgers with Worcestershire sauce and an extra helping of coleslaw, she would stop me and wink, saying, "I remember, Mr. Picky."

Each night I gave her the lovey eyes. But the problem was, Betty was pregnant. She was only five-and-a-half feet tall with rail-thin arms and legs, yet she looked as though she was carrying triplets. I cursed my luck I hadn't known her before she'd found her man. It got me down, even, and whenever Betty left with our orders I would settle into the mopes. Finally one of the fellas on the construction team told me to buck up and ask her on a date.

"It would never work," I conceded. "There's already a luckier man than me."

"Look at her finger, numbnuts." That fella held out his hand, knuckles toward me, over the Formica tabletop. "No ring. Open your eyes, numbnuts. She might got one in the oven, but that don't mean some dope's got his gas line screwed in her backside."

All through dinner that night my head and heart were in a tizzy. Once we paid and the other boys left, I waited. She came to bus our dishes, and I told her my name was Carl.

"Oh," she said.

"Yeah," I said. "Carl. What's your name?"

She tapped an index finger against her nametag. "Betty. You knew that."

I told her it was a pretty name. I said with her long black hair twisted to the side in a braid, she looked nothing like Betty in the Archie comics. And we kept talking. Sometimes I made her laugh, and she leaned forward and smiled and touched my elbow.

Soon the boys in the pickup honked at me to get moving.

"Say, Betty," I said. "Maybe you already got some dude, some dude that takes good care of you, or maybe your boyfriend, who's probably a righteous fellow—"

"I don't have a boyfriend," she interrupted. "You want to go out some time?"

I said, "Yes!"

That weekend she took me out in North Platte, which was her hometown. We went to a honky-tonk, where a group of mandolin and fiddle players had the stage. Betty and I danced, but she kept her distance, red-faced and glistening because of the pregnancy. Eventually she leaned in and said, "Let's rest." We sat beside each other in a vinyl booth, ordered two root beers, and listened to the music. Then she said, "Carl, can I tell you something? You promise you won't run away?"

"Of course," I said. "I promise."

"I'm not really pregnant." She waited for my reaction. After time passed and I hadn't looked away from her belly, she said, "It's just a suit. So I can milk bigger tips at the diner, so customers treat me with more sympathy. Even my boss knows. No one catches on, because all our customers are transients like you."

"Is there a baby in it?" I asked.

"No. It's just a suit. It's made of foam."

"You're not pregnant?"

"No, Carl. Here." She took my hand and pressed it against her soft foam stomach. Then she lifted the side of her blouse, revealing flesh-colored padding and some elastic straps.

"You trickster," I said. "You tricked me! I've been leaving you twenty-five percent."

She gave me a cute look. Then she unfastened her suit and tossed it under the table, and she and I cut it up on the dance floor until long after the musicians had left the stage.

In time we got married and I made her pregnant for real with Carl Jr. But it wasn't until Betty reached her third trimester that I remembered about that old suit. Suddenly I was on deadline to cook up a snappy joke. Finally, when we were driving away from Camden Yards after an Orioles game, she told me her water had broke.

"Nice try, Betty," I said. "You've been playing this game ever since we met."

"Carl, get in the left lane. We need to go to the hospital. Left lane, Carl."

"Fool me once," I said.

"Carl, change lanes. Now! Change lanes, Carl. You're going home but we need the hospital. Carl! Change! Lanes! Listen to me!"

"Uh huh. Do me a favor, Betty." I looked away from the road and into her eyes. "Bring me my Worcestershire burger and coleslaw on the double." Then I swung the wheel and turned onto the ramp toward the hospital. I looked at her again, and she was smiling. I tricked her!

Eventually the Art Institute put me on such stringent academic probation that I knew it was senseless to continue. I withdrew. For several months I was unemployed and without purpose. Often I found myself parked on the loveseat, my mind drifting for some reason to the image of a golden eagle with the head of an alligator. Who knows what started this line of thinking? But I let it take its course. I pictured this eagle-alligator inhabiting the coastal mountains, a pacifist, maybe even a vegetarian, its day-to-day activity protecting hikers from bears, mountain lions, and perverts. In time I began to think of it as the eaglegator.

Thoughts of the eaglegator were bouncing around my skull one afternoon when Trevor Thomas entered my front door with a plastic sack of fruit and several bags of ice. "Hey Carl. I need to use your blender. Do you have a blender?"

I shook my head no, absently.

"Ground control to Major Tom. What's going on, space cadet?"

"Lately I've been having a lot of thoughts." I looked up to Trevor Thomas. "About a mythical bird."

Trevor Thomas put down his bags. He lowered himself to the floor and sat cross-legged, like a kid at story hour. "Do tell."

"To start," I said, "imagine a sea swell washing an alligator egg into a golden eagle nest at Big Sur. Then imagine the mother eagle adopting it and raising it as her own." Upon hatching, it was clear this child was different. Where his brothers and sisters had feathers, he had scales and spines. Where they flew with grace and majesty, he fluttered clumsily and botched his landings. The eaglegator's youth was awkward and often painful. Yet in time he gained coordination, confidence. When the fog rolled in from the Pacific Ocean he used his large jaw to prune his clan's feathers, and during hatching season he built nests of heavy logs at the tops of the tallest redwoods. He came to accept his uniqueness as a virtue. As new generations emerged, the eaglegator transformed into an elder, although he chose to live alone.

My tale went on for a good half-hour. When I finished Trevor Thomas said, "Yes. The eaglegator! I can see it now." He was bouncing his knees like a seesaw and wringing his hands before his chest. "She can fly underwater, she can swim in the air."

"Well, I never said that."

"She has alligator claws, but on the claws are eagle talons."

"It's a he, I was thinking." Despite Trevor Thomas's suggestions, I was thrilled he'd enjoyed my idea. I felt unburdened, like after telling the eaglegator's story I could now move onto other, more productive thoughts.

Yet Trevor Thomas wanted to know more. Was there an arch-enemy? What was the approximate wingspan? Did it speak English? Mexican? Bear language? These were issues I hadn't considered. Finally I noticed that his bags of ice were draining across on the hardwood floor.

"Is the eaglegator immortal?" he asked.

"What are you doing with that ice?" I said.

He looked at the large puddle and jumped to his feet. "Oh, nuts! Gotta go." He tapped an index finger against his temple. "Good thinking, Carl. Love it." Then he left with his plastic sack of fruit and what was left of those bags of ice.

I soon forgot about the eaglegator. After I left the Institute, my federal loan got rescinded and I found myself in egregious debt. To make ends meet, I pawned my Moog and four-track and took work as a landscaping grunt. The job was humiliating: my nose went pink with sunburn, I was always hungry, and the boys on the crew would burp out vulgarities and chuck dirt at each other's crotches for a joke. In the evenings I returned home covered in earth and fell straight to sleep without bathing.

One night Trevor Thomas was waiting on my front step. As was usual during this stretch, I was tired and regrettably irritable, and only wanted to collapse onto my loveseat.

"Good news, Carl, old boy!"

"I'm in the mood for good news," I said, unlocking my door and stepping into the living room. "You don't mind if I sit down, do you? I'm pooped."

"Please do. Get comfortable." He shut the door and took a deep breath. "Okay. Number one: What is the nickname of San Francisco's professional football franchise?"

"The Forty-Niners," I said, untying my boots and loosening my shirt collar.

"Yes. Now, why are they called the Forty-Niners?"

"Gold Rush of 1849."

"Two for two, Carl. Lastly, what does a Forty-Niner look like?"

I pondered the question. But I didn't know. Whatever it was, it was red and gold. Thinking it might be a trick, I said, "A winner. It looks like a winner."

Trevor Thomas went silent for a time. Then he said, "Okay, partial credit. The correct answer was, 'I don't know.' But here—" He reached into his back pocket and handed me a folded sheet of paper. "Here's what it will look like from now on."

The paper showed a lithograph with three lines curving upward in a half-circle, and below those lines a silhouette of snow-capped mountain peaks. Flying between the curved lines and the peaks was a caricature I knew immediately to be the eaglegator. It was pretty much how I'd described it to Trevor Thomas, except its eyes were bulgy and altogether too large. Its eyes made it look garish and cartoony.

I handed the paper back to Trevor Thomas.

He pushed it back to me.

"I'll explain." He plopped down beside me on the loveseat. "These three lines: This first one, it's for Trevor Thomas. That's me. This second one, it's for Carl—what's your last name, Carl?"

"Lehmann."

"For Carl Lehmann." He paused. "Really, Lehmann? It's hard to say those two L's in a row. And this third line, it's for the eaglegator. The mountaintops and the beast are self-explanatory."

I scrutinized the lithograph. I disapproved, and my face showed it.

"Hear me out, old boy," he said. "These three lines will run down the middle of the helmet. On both sides will be decals with the mountains and the beast."

"He's not a beast," I said.

"Imagine it: the San Francisco Forty-Niners, carried on the wings of an eagle, protected by the teeth of an alligator, running like the wind, um, blocking like the mountains. I don't know. I just made that up. But listen, first we need to spread the myth. I was thinking you'd write the words, I'd storyboard a comic book. 'Birth of the Eaglegator.' You with me, Carl? I told the suits at Candlestick I'd have a mockup ready by next week."

"No," I moaned. "Did you send this out?"

He pointed to the letterhead, which read, TREVOR & KARL. "Why you looking at me like that? I ordered three boxes of this stationery. I thought you'd be tickled."

"No," I told him. "I'm not tickled. I never asked for this."

"You know what, Carl? You are being a first-rate negative nancy. You know as well as I do there's no such thing as a Forty-Niner. But there'll always be the Forty-Niner eaglegator beast, staring down opponents and bringing inspiration to the city."

"Quit calling him a beast," I snapped. "The eaglegator's a friendly creature—you know that, Trevor Thomas. In his heart he's only trying to find out where he belongs."

"But it needs to be intimidating. You can't have a softie on a football helmet." He began pacing the room, looking between me and the lithographed paper. "How about this? We'll compromise: he'll have the appearance of being dangerous, but he'll be on the helmets, which keep players safe."

"Darnit, Trevor," I shouted, "you're not listening! This wasn't what I wanted. You take my name off there!"

I picked up one of my boots and slammed the heel on the floor. Trevor Thomas quit pacing and looked me over. He had never seen me so angry. I don't know that I had ever been, or would ever be, so angry.

"Fine, Carl. I'll take your name off." He held out the lithographed sheet, carefully tore off the karl and tossed it to the floor. "You want out, you got it. The idea's mine now."

"Good. Leave me alone, Trevor Thomas."

"I will. You're on your own, Carl." He stuffed the sheet in his back pocket. "When you come crawling back, remember this night. Any communication you got, you can talk to my lawyer. In fact, talk to my lawyer's lawyer. We're too busy to mess around with negativity."

He stormed out, slamming the door behind himself.

And that's where things ended, the talk of the eaglegator and my friendship with Trevor Thomas. I entered a huff that lasted several days. At my worst I posted a handmade sign on my front door that read, NO TREVOR THOMASES'S ALLOWED. Neither of us were ones to hold a grudge, but he never came around after that, even once I removed the sign.

By the time I had forgotten our spat, I'd also somewhat forgotten Trevor Thomas. It must have been the same for him. Our memories of each other slowly diminished.

I don't recall any singular incident that made me know I should leave San Francisco. It was just one of those feelings in my gut. Suddenly everything had changed, and nothing was familiar. Among other things, my mother, who was eighty years old and had been living in a nursing home back in Alameda, passed away. She'd had me while in her fifties. My two older brothers and my sister were separated from me by twenty years. Except for my sister, who took care of me while I was young but then disappeared and cut off contact, my siblings and I had never known each other. With my mother gone, I realized I was alone in northern California, maybe alone in the world.

I left town without saying good-bye to anyone. Just one night I was gone, no explanation given. How could I have done that? If I remember correctly, my lease had expired and at the time it seemed as good a reason as any.

Why am I thinking about all this now? Because last week I received a message on the email from Debbie Beecham, which said that Trevor Thomas had been killed in a boating accident on San Francisco Bay.

I found this entirely shocking. First of all, I had forgotten about Trevor Thomas. His whereabouts and whatabouts had eluded me. And second, I didn't know who Debbie Beecham was, or how she got my computer address.

Because I believed the whole thing to be a joke, I printed the message and put it in my briefcase to take home and show Betty. But I forgot, because my briefcase serves as little else than a lunchbox. It wasn't until Friday morning, when Betty was packing my lunch, that she finally asked what was the story with Debbie Beecham's message. I said I was hoping she could tell me.

"Debbie's that nice woman from the farmers' market," she said. "You remember your argument at the dunking booth."

This I did remember. Last fall Betty and I stuck Carl Jr. on a Boy Scout trip and drove down to a farmers' market in Annapolis—a large, diverse farmers' market, almost like a fair. As we were walking the midway, a man called to me from the seat of a Rotary Club dunking booth, "Hey featherweight, with the purdy wife. Let's see that arm, Sally." His words struck me as rude, and in a fit of pride I bought three softballs from the ticket woman. It was a bad idea. This man heckled me mercilessly, for I'd never been taught to throw. After my second ball arced high over the target, he cackled, "Try it underhand, Nancy."

"You watch your mouth," I shouted back.

We then exchanged a series of unkind words, to the point where I refused to throw the final softball. It became a serious tiff. Several lookyloos stopped to check on the fuss.

Betty pulled me aside and told me to cool it, mister, when some lady in a pantsuit approached and said, "Carl? Carl Lehmann?" It was Debbie Beecham, although I didn't recognize her. She introduced herself to Betty and explained how she and I had been friends back in San Francisco. Then I recalled how Debbie Beecham had drifted through our random groupings, a kind girl who occasionally, unfortunately, got plain out of her head. Back then her tangled hair reached down to her waist, and she wore enough bead jewelry that she clicked with every motion. Now here we were, both in our fifties at a farmers' market on the other side of the country, and I had just narrowly avoided a scuffle.

"We lost touch after you left San Francisco," Debbie Beecham said to me. "It was like one day you had simply vanished."

"This is true," I said.

"So what's become of you these days? How have you been, Carl?"

I told her I work at Assurance Tax Services, and me and Betty have lived in Greater Baltimore almost twenty years now. It's been good to us. We're happy and healthy and lucky, insured and free of debt. Our house was appreciating in value, and that summer we'd been playing badminton in the backyard. We have a kid, and Betty was thinking she might run for School Board. Life, as I explained it to Debbie Beecham, was a simple and satisfying matter.

Betty was packing my lunch when she reminded me about Debbie Beecham. Then she asked about Trevor Thomas. But I had to leave for work, so I kissed her good-bye and promised we would talk that night. (Carl Jr. responded to our kiss with a vulgar retching noise, the scamp.)

But how was I to explain to Betty about Trevor Thomas? Believe it or not, she and I had hardly discussed our respective pasts. With her I had started anew. I'd become someone different from California Carl, although I still had affection for that time and place. How could I narrate my history when the details are so jumbled in my mind?

These memories—you can't hold them in your hand. Blink and they're gone! In my life I've seen many places and known many people, but given time I forget they even exist. Even the little mementos, the fliers and letters and glitter, they're probably scattered across some rotten landfill, their scraps blowing gradually into the bay. Or of the 500 copies of *Best Sogs*, I'd be lucky if even one isn't smashed up and forgotten. I don't have a copy but I wish to the stars I did. I would play it for Betty and say, Snickers, this is who I was back then.

When I returned from work, Betty was in the kitchen warming milk for my hot cocoa. "Hey mister," she said, "you look like you're in a cloud. What gives?"

"I had a crummy day," I said, handing her my briefcase. "My focus was out the window. I got lost in some odd thoughts."

"Oh, Carl." She put her hand on my elbow. "Take your time. We've got all weekend." This was right—we'd sent Carl Jr.to a math camp or a swimming meet somewhere around D.C., and the weekend was mine and Betty's.

"I want to tell you everything," I said, "but I don't know how to say it."

She waited for me to continue.

"Trevor Thomas was a guy I used to be friends with."

"I know, Carl. I called Debbie this afternoon. Here."

She handed me the mug of cocoa and led me by the hand into our den, where we sat beside each other on the sofa. She told me about her phone call with Debbie Beecham.

Trevor Thomas had eventually been booted from the Art Institute, after which he took odd jobs here and there, painting houses, moving office equipment, laying down the yellow stripes on the highway. Nothing seemed to stick. Later in life he grappled with panic and despair, and to combat these feelings he would set out fishing on a secondhand pontoon. He didn't mind going it alone. One day he was out off Gashouse Cove and something happened, a gust of wind, or maybe he fell asleep. No one's sure. There was no foul play, no drugs or alcohol involved. And Trevor Thomas had hardly anyone in his life at the end. He's buried up in Marin County, not far at all across the Golden Gate Bridge, in a plot beside his parents, who apparently had been gone as long as I'd known him.

I think about death sometimes, though I don't discuss it with Betty. And I think it's only like going to sleep: your eyelids feel heavy and begin to droop, and you might kick your legs or give a little snort, then in an instant you've faded into dreams. The end. But for Trevor Thomas, who drowned, it must have been like when you're at a party with everyone you know and trust, where everything's familiar and you feel safe. You let loose, finding your rhythm, until you notice it's early and you've been overdoing it, and unless you turn back now you're facing the blackout. Yet you think, *I've done this before, I know my limits*, and soon enough what started as a shade of gray becomes total black pitch darkness.

"Debbie said you used to play guitar."

"I played bass guitar. Some other things, too."

Betty clasped my hand as we sat together on the sofa.

"What did Trevor play?"

"I don't remember him being into music. But he was keen at drawing, and at making lithographs."

For a time Betty and I were silent in each other's company. Then I said, "He was an idea man." She gave a look of encouragement, so I set my mug on the end table and continued. "Back then I lived in the Mission District, and Trevor Thomas was just across the alley. I would watch from my ratty old loveseat while he held court in my living room."

I went on, and one description led to the next—Minty Coke, Bring Mays Back, the Golden Gate Monster, and that whole stink over the eaglegator. Soon I was on my feet, acting out scenes and putting on voices. Betty pulled her legs underneath herself on the sofa. "Slow down, Carl," she said. "You're rattling on so fast I can barely keep up." But I'd been set loose like a whirlwind, rambling forward, my mouth hardly keeping pace with my mind. Shadows rolled across the den, until the sky outside turned dark with night.

When I finally dropped back onto the sofa, Betty leaned into me and said, "I wish I had a chance to know Trevor." Yes, I said, he made himself known. And I had the urge to keep talking, to keep on telling stories. But I couldn't think of any I hadn't just told her.

I know there's more!

Slow Duo

Stephen Kopel

Knuckles of wind
      punch late blossoms,
            petals pirouette
                and my grandmothers,
                    elbows linked,
                          shuffle their Thursday ballet
                        around the park's perimeter,
                  flowers garland
              frosted curls,
          feisty broads
      without partners
on stage one more season

kindly hold your applause

Contributors

Erick Aare lives near Gaston, Oregon and attended Portland State University.

Ruth Beck is a writer born and raised in rural, coastal western Oregon. She holds a degree in Religion and Philosophy with a minor in Creative Writing from Marylhurst University, where she was the recipient of the Binford Writing Award. Her poetry has appeared in a handful of literary journals. Ruth lives with her husband and son in their 120-year old farmhouse, and works on her family's sheep and tree farm where she makes artisan soaps.

A lifelong New Englander, **Jeff Bernstein** divides his time between Boston and Central Vermont. Recent poems appeared or are forthcoming in *The Aurorean, Ballard Street Poetry Journal, Hobble Creek Review, Loch Raven Review, Main Street Rag, Penny Ante Feud, Route Seven: A Vermont Literary Journal, San Pedro River Review,* and *Thrush.* His poem "A Short Guide to the Proper Treatment of Maryland Blue Crabs" was a semi-finalist in the *Naugatuck River Review* 2010 Narrative Poetry Contest. His chapbook, *Interior Music* was published by Foothills Publishing in 2010. Jeff's writer's blog can be found hurricanelodge.com

Rachel Squires Bloom's poems have appeared in *The Hawaii Review, Poet Lore, Fugue, Poetry East, Kimera, Nomad's Choir, The Mad Poet's Review, Bluster, 96 Inc., Bellowing Ark, Slugfest, Thin Air,*

Taproot Literary Review, True Romance, Lucid Stone, and *Green Hills Literary Lantern.* Two of her poems have been nominated for the Pushcart Prize. She holds Master's degrees in English Literature and Education and a Doctorate in Educational Leadership. She teaches in Quincy, Massachusetts.

Doug Bolling's poetry has appeared in *Georgetown Review, Blue Unicorn, Marginalia, Slant, Oregon East, Wallace Stevens Journal, English Journal, Bluestem, Italian Americana, Cider Press Review,* and *Connecticut River Review,* among others. He was the featured poet in the January 2011 issue of *Flowers & Vortexes* and has received two Pushcart nominations. He lives in Flossmoor, Illinois, outside Chicago.

For the moment, **John F. Buckley** lives in Orange County, California. His work has been published in a number of places, one of which nominated him for a Pushcart Prize in 2009. His chapbook Breach Birth was published on Propaganda Press in March 2011. His full-length collaboration with Martin Ott, *Poets' Guide to America,* is coming out on Brooklyn Arts Press in summer 2012.

Tracy Burkholder's writing has appeared or is forthcoming in *Cincinnati Review, Portland Review, Silk Road,* and *Pacific Review* as well as the anthology *Our Portland Story, Vol. 2.* She received her MFA from Bennington College and lives in Portland, OR.

John Randolph Carter is a poet and artist. A finalist for the National Poetry Series, his poetry has appeared in journals including *Bomb, The Cream City Review, LIT, Margie, North American Review, The*

Pinch, *Verse*, and *Washington Square*. He has been the recipient of NEA, New York State Council, and Fulbright grants. His art is in thirty-two public collections including the Metropolitan Museum of Art. One-person exhibitions include The University of Michigan Art Museum and the Minneapolis Institute.

R.T. Castleberry is a widely published poet and social critic. He was a co-founder of the Flying Dutchman Writers Troupe, co-editor/publisher of the poetry magazine *Curbside Review*, an assistant editor for *Lily Poetry Review* and *Ardent*. His work has appeared most recently in *Comstock Review*, *Green Mountains Review*, *The Alembic*, *Paterson Literary Review*, *Caveat Lector*, *Perigee*, *Silk Road*, and *Argestes*. He was a finalist for the 2008 Arts & Letters/Rumi Prize for Poetry. His chapbook, *Arriving At The Riverside*, was published by Finishing Line Press in January, 2010. An e-book, *Dialogue and Appetite*, was published by Right Hand Pointing in May, 2011.

James Deahl was born in Pittsburgh in 1945. He grew up in there, as well as the Laurel Highlands region of the Appalachian Mountains. He moved to Canada in 1970 and now lives in Sarnia. He is the author of twenty literary titles. His three most recent books are: *North of Belleville*, *Opening The Stone Heart*, and *No Star Is Lost*.

Retired from teaching children with special needs, **Susan Duke** manages a storage facility with her husband, three adult children, and two grandsons. She enjoys reading, writing, and her morning one mile walks.

David Harris Ebenbach's first book of short stories, *Between Camelots* (University of Pittsburgh Press), won the Drue Heinz Literature Prize and the GLCA New Writer's Award. His second book, a guide to creativity called *The Artist's Torah*, is forthcoming from Cascade Books. His poetry has appeared in, among other places, *Beloit Poetry Journal*, *Subtropics*, and *Hayden's Ferry Review*. Recently awarded fellowships to the MacDowell Colony and the Vermont Studio Center and an Individual Excellence Award from the Ohio Arts Council, Ebenbach has a PhD in Psychology from the University of Wisconsin-Madison and an MFA in Writing from Vermont College. He teaches at Georgetown University and George Washington University. Find out more at www.davidebenbach.com.

Don Eckler first began writing poetry in a journal given to him by his 4th year high school English teacher. A retired Master Chief of the US Coast Guard, Don received his BS degree from Black Hills State University, and served in the Peace Corps in the Fiji Islands.

Jean Esteve lives in Waldport, Oregon, likes dogs, and enjoys swimming. New work is scheduled for publication in *Freshwater*, *Mudfish*, and *Pearl*.

Colette Fallon is a fine art oil painter living in a suburb of Portland, Oregon. Her range of work includes landscapes, seascapes, portraits, and still life. Her work has been featured in various galleries in Oregon and she has received awards for her work. She has also done commission work for interested parties and has been painting for over 30 years. Living in the Pacific Northwest has given her a wealth of subject matter. Colette is also a composer. She has a CD of her music and a music video of one of her compositions. She is currently working on another music project as well as continuing her painting endeavors.

Brandi George's work has recently appeared or is forthcoming in *Nimrod International Journal*, *Gulf Coast*, *Prairie Schooner*, *Best New Poets 2010*, and elsewhere. She currently resides in Tallahassee, Florida, where she teaches writing.

Arthur Gottlieb is an Oregon poet whose work has appeared in many small literary magazines, including *The Ledge*, *Chiron Review*, *The Alembic*, *The Pacific Review*, *Lullwater Review*, and many others.

Danielle Hanson received her MFA from Arizona State University and now lives in Atlanta, GA. Her work has appeared in over 40 journals and anthologies, including *Hubbub*, *Iodine*, *Lake Effect*, *Rosebud*, *The Cortland Review*, *Poet Lore*, *Asheville Poetry Review*, and *Blackbird*. She has edited *Hayden's Ferry Review*, been on staff at The Meacham Writers' Conference and received the Fulton County Arts Council Grant for a residency at the Hambidge Center.

Lisa Ohlen Harris lives and works in Newberg, Oregon, where the annual rainfall averages more than 40 inches. She is the author of the Middle East memoir *Through the Veil*, which was a finalist for the 2011 Oregon Book Award.

Kait Heacock is a recent transplant to Portland, Oregon, having grown up in Central Washington and spending the last six years in Seattle. She is a graduate student at Portland State University working on a Master's in Book Publishing. She has been writing short fiction for most of her life and earned her BA in English from Seattle Pacific University. Her greatest literary influence is Raymond Carver. She admires his unique combination of brevity and intensity. They also happen to be from the same hometown.

Joseph Holt works in bridge maintenance around northeastern South Dakota and teaches at the University of Minnesota. His fiction has recently appeared in *Gulf Coast* and *New Ohio Review*.

Rich Ives is the 2009 winner of the Francis Locke Memorial Poetry Award from *Bitter Oleander* and the 2012 winner of the Creative Nonfiction Prize from *Thin Air* magazine. The Spring 2011 *Bitter Oleander* contains a feature including an interview and 18 of his hybrid works.

William Jolliff serves as professor of English at George Fox University. He has published critical articles and poems in over a hundred periodicals, including *Northwest Review*, *Southern Humanities Review*, *Midwest Quarterly*, *Christianity and Literature*, and *Appalachian Journal*. His most recent poetry chapbook is *Searching for a White Crow* (2009).

Tanque R. Jones lives in Knoxville, TN, where she earned her BA from the University of Tennessee. She is currently writing a book of poems, a novel and a collection of essays while she earns her MFA.

Sara Kirschenbaum is a writer and artist in Portland, Oregon. She has been published in *Calyx*, *Fiction International*, *J Journal*, *Kalliope*, *Mothering Magazine*, *The Oregonian*, *Poetica*, *Portland Parent*, the *Portland Tribune*, and other publications. She has been a guest commentator for NPR's Marketplace and has published on Salon.com.

She is currently seeking a publisher for her memoir about postpartum OCD. She can be reached through her website: sarakirschenbaum. com.

Stephen Kopel is a teacher, cyclist, art collector, civic benefactor and a working wordsmith. Author of chapbooks *crux* and *crax*, as well as novel *Spritz*, his work resides in *Margie*, *The Evansville Review*, *Aethlon*, *Main Street Rag*, *Harpur Palate*, and *Antigonish Review*. The poet invests in the 'take stock market' with assets allocated in straight talk, caring and courage. Contact: stephen.kopel@live.com

Haesong Kwon was born in Incheon, Korea, but has lived most of his life in the states. Presently, he lives in Stillwater, OK, and pursues a PhD in English at Oklahoma State University. He's an assistant editor at the *Cimmarron Review*, and has poems in *Roger*, *Red Rock Review*, *Oxford Magazine*, and others.

Teresa Lane, 19, is a freshman at WSU Vancouver majoring in journalism. She has been honored with an award for her poetry from the Nature of Words Rising Stars writing competition in Bend, Oregon. Her short story work has been nationally recognized through the YoungARTS program. She is very excited to be part of this edition of the *Clackamas Literary Review*.

Eric le Fatte graduated from MIT with a BS in Biology; went to graduate school at Northeastern University in English Literature; worked as the Returns King at Eastern Mountain Sports; and returned to MIT to receive a PhD in Biology. He currently teaches, backpacks, and writes in the Portland, Oregon area. His poems have appeared in *The Moun-*

tain Gazette, Rune, Windfall, and *The Raven Chronicles.* He has been known to answer emails addressed to elef1234@gmail.com.

Robert Levy's work has appeared in *Poetry, Paris Review, Georgia Review, Southern Review,* and many others. New work is in, or forthcoming in, *Alaska Quarterly Review, Southwest Review, River Styx,* and *Tar River Poetry.* He is a past winner of an NEA Fellowship and has published two full-length collections, *Whistle Maker* (Anhinga) and *In the Century of Small Gestures* (Defined Providence), as well as four chapbooks.

Jack e Lorts is a retired educator living in Fossil, Oregon. After several years as School Superintendent, he now serves as Mayor of Fossil. His poems have appeared widely, if infrequently, over the past 40+ years in such places as *Arizona Quarterly, Kansas Quarterly, English Journal, Fireweed, Fishtrap, Oregon English, High Desert Journal* (upcoming), *Arsenic Lobster,* and others. Two chapbooks are out from Pudding House and *Dear Gilbert Sorrentino & Other Poems* from Finishing Line Press this past year. Forthcoming from Pudding House later this year is *The Love Songs of Ephram Pratt.*

Rebecca Macijeski received her Bachelor's degree in English and Music from Simmons College in Boston, and earned her MFA in Poetry from Vermont College of Fine Arts in 2011. Her lifelong studies of classical violin and writing have prompted travel to such countries as Austria, Slovenia, and Japan. She currently serves as assistant poetry editor for *Hunger Mountain.*

America Marie lives, works, and writes in Portland, Oregon. She loves gardening, travel, and Scottie dogs. Her writing has appeared in *Poetry Motel* and *Analekta*.

Rick Marlatt's first book, *How We Fall Apart*, was the winner of the Seven Circle Press Poetry Award. He is a graduate of the MFA program at the University of California, Riverside, where he served as poetry editor of the *Coachella Review*. His poems have appeared widely in print and online publications including *Rattling Wall*, *New York Quarterly*, and *Midway*. Recently, his criticism has appeared in *The New York Times*, *Poetry Magazine*, and *Rattle*. Read more at rickmarlatt.com.

Erica Woiwode Mason is a teacher, classical pianist, and poet, among other things. Her work has been published in *Turbula*, *ArtisticRights*, *Academic Exchange*, *The Poetry Conspiracy*, and *L.A. Miscellany*. Erica was born and raised in San Diego, California, and now lives in Portland, Oregon with her husband and son. She teaches at Clackamas Community College.

Susan H. Maurer has had 6 chapbooks published and her full-length work *Perfect Dark* was published by Ungovernable Press out of Sweden.

Jean McDonough was born in Omaha, Nebraska and now resides in upstate New York. She earned an MFA from Rainier Writers Workshop at Pacific Lutheran University and was the recipient of the 1995 Academy of American Poets Prize. Her work has appeared in *Dos Passos Review*, *Cold Mountain Review*, *The American Literary Review*,

Quarterly West, Tar River Poetry, Salamander, Bayou, and *Poet Lore* among others. Her poem, "June, Maybe" is forthcoming in *The Untidy Season: An Anthology of Nebraska Women Poets* by Backwaters Press.

M.E. Mitchell is a former thoroughbred trainer who divides her time between downstate New York and historic Saratoga Springs. After leaving the racing industry, she focused on writing again in addition to earning a BS in Communications and a MA in Sports Management. Her fiction, gleaned from those years at various racetracks, has appeared or is forthcoming in *The Other Herald, Bumble Jacket Miscellany, Down in the Dirt, A Few Lines Magazine,* and *The Threshold,* among others.

After teaching for nearly 30 years in Grinnell College's Writing Lab, **Betty Moffett** has turned her attention to her own writing—and developed real sympathy for her students. Her stories, poems, and essays have appeared in various magazines and journals, including *The MacGuffin, Limestone, The Licking River Review, The Grinnell Magazine,* and *The Wapsipinicon Almanac.* She and her husband live on a farm in Iowa and play with the Too Many String Band.

Paul Nelson was for years a Professor and Director of Creative Writing for Ohio University, and has six books out. These include an AWP Winner, and a University of Alabama Press Series Selection. A new book, *Burning the Furniture,* is forthcoming with Guernica Editions. An NEA Fellow, he lives and writes now from the North Shore of O'ahu where trolling miles out is like writing poetry, waiting for a strike by something natural.

James B. Nicola has had over two hundred poems appear in publications including *Tar River*, the *Texas Review*, *The Lyric*, and *Nimrod*. A stage director by profession, his book *Playing the Audience* won a CHOICE Award. He also won the Dana Literary Award for poetry, was nominated for a Rhysling Award, and was a featured poet at *The New Formalist* in 2010. His first chapbook of poems, *Still*, will be out in 2012 from Stasia Press.

Stanley Morris Noah has a BGS degree from The University of Texas at Dallas. His work has been published in the following: *Wisconsin Review*, *Nexus*, *Cottonwood*, *South Carolina Review*, *Poetry Nottingham*, and other publications in the U.S.A., Britain, Canada, and New Zealand.

Dan O'Brien's poems have appeared in *Alaska Quarterly Review*, *Crab Orchard Review*, *Greensboro Review*, and elsewhere. His play *The Body of an American*, about the haunting of war reporter Paul Watson, is the winner of the 2011 L. Arnold Weissberger Award and will premiere at Portland Center Stage in 2012. Website: danobrien.org

Simon Perchik is an attorney whose poems have appeared in *Partisan Review*, *The New Yorker*, and elsewhere. For more information, including his essay "Magic, Illusion and Other Realities" and a complete bibliography, please visit his website at simonperchik.com.

Dylan Dean Plotner is a student at Clackamas Community College, working on his Associate's degree, focusing on writing and literature. His hope is to become a successful fiction writer. He enjoys writing inspiring and passionate stories and poems.

Connie Post served as the first Poet Laureate of Livermore, California from 2005- 2009. Her work has appeared in *The Aurorean, Calyx, Kalliope, Cold Mountain Review, Chiron Review, Crab Creek Review, Comstock Review, DMQ Review, Dogwood, The Great American Poetry Show, The Pedestal Magazine, Slipstream*, and *The Toronto Quarterly*. She was the winner of the Cover Prize for the Spring 2009 issue of *The Dirty Napkin* and the winner of the 2009 Caesura Poetry Awards from The Poetry Center of San Jose. Her most recent book *Trip Wires* was released in September 2010, and received praise from Al Young, California's former Poet Laureate.

Jack Powers lives in Fairfield, Connecticut with his wife and three children and teaches at Joel Barlow High School in nearby Redding. His poems have appeared in *Rattle, Poet Lore, Cortland Review, Inkwell*, and elsewhere.

Lee Rossi's latest book is *Wheelchair Samurai*. His poems, reviews, and interviews have appeared in *The Harvard Review, Poetry Northwest, The Beloit Poetry Journal*, and *The Southern Poetry Review*. He is a staff reviewer and interviewer for the online magazine *Pedestal*. He lives in the San Francisco Bay Area. His assets consist solely of used clothing and some rapidly depreciating poems, and he is still waiting for his government bailout. If you're as troubled as he is and know where his TARP funds went, please contact ghostdiarist@yahoo.com.

Andrea Scarpino is the author of the chapbook *The Grove Behind* (Finishing Line Press) and a forthcoming full-length collection from Red Hen Press. She received an MFA in Creative Writing from The Ohio State University, has been nominated for a Pushcart Prize, and teaches with Union Institute and University's Cohort PhD program in Interdisciplinary Studies. She is a weekly contributor for the blog "Planet of the Blind."

Peter Serchuk's poems have appeared in a variety of journals big and small including *Boulevard*, *Poetry*, *Denver Quarterly*, *North American Review*, *Texas Review*, *South Carolina Review*, *New York Quarterly* and others. A new collection, *All That Remains*, is forthcoming from WordTech Editions. He lives in Los Angeles, California.

Kristen Svenson is an author, publisher, and adventurer living in Portland, Oregon. She studied English at Willamette University and earned her Master's degree in writing and book publishing at Portland State University. Her poetry and short stories have appeared in various national journals and anthologies.

Michael Torok lives in Austin, Texas with his son. He has a day job as community strategist and director for a software company and looks forward to the infrequent times he is unplugged from the grid. He received his PhD in English from ULL in 1999 and has been previously published in *Fox Cry Review*, *Louisiana Review*, and *Red Rock Review*, among others. His first book of poetry, *Goodbyes are Hellos*, is due out in 2012.

Dennis Vannatta has published stories in many magazines and anthologies, including *Chariton Review*, *Boulevard*, *Antioch Review*, and *Pushcart XV*. He also has three collections: *This Time, This Place* and *Prayers for the Dead*, both by White Pine Press, and *Lives of the Artists* by Livingston Press. His newest collection, *Rockaway Children: Stories*, is forthcoming from Rising Star Press.

Visit

CLR
CLACKAMAS LITERARY REVIEW

clackamasliteraryreview.org
facebook.com/clackamasliteraryreview

Contact
clr@clackamas.edu

CLACKAMAS LITERARY REVIEW

the finest writing for the best readers

Clackamas Literary Review has been committed to bringing you the best writing from around the world since 1997. Subscribe now to receive the latest and forthcoming issues.

Clackamas Literary Review

_____ 1 year $10

_____ 2 years $18

_____ 3 years $26

Name _____

Address _____

City / State / Zip _____

Email _____

Send this form and check or money order to:

Clackamas Literary Review
English Department
Clackamas Community College
19600 Molalla Avenue
Oregon City, Oregon 97045

www.ingramcontent.com/pod-product-compliance
Lightning Source LLC
Chambersburg PA
CBHW071459170626
46811CB00007B/2640